Manufacturing Guilt

Manufacturing Guilt

Wrongful Convictions in Canada

B ARRIE A NDERSON WITH D AWN A NDERSON

Fernwood Publishing • Halifax

Editing: Doug Smith
Cover photo: Maggier Murray
Design and production: Beverley Rach
Printed and bound in Canada by: Hignell Printing Limited

A publication of:
Fernwood Publishing
Box 9409, Station A
Halifax, Nova Scotia
B3K 5S3

Fernwood Publishing Company Limited gratefully acknowledges the financial support of the Ministry of Canadian Heritage and the Nova Scotia Department of Education and Culture.

Third printing August 2001

Canadian Cataloguing in Publication Data

Anderson, Barrie

Manufacturing Guilt

Includes bibliographical references.
ISBN 1-895686-93-8

1. Judicial error -- Canada. 2. False imprisonment -- Canada.
I. Anderson, Dawn. II. Title.

KE9440.A84 1997   347.71012   C97-950232-2

Contents

Dedication

To our mothers, Dorothy and Joyce

Acknowledgements

Many people played a part in the production of this book and we wish to thank them all. In particular, we are indebted to Brian Anderson, David Anderson, Dorothy Anderson, Joyce Anderson, Stephen Brickey, Elizabeth Comack, Cheryl Heinemann, Daniel Levis, Mark LaRocque and Flo Rolls for their valuable suggestions during the various drafts of the manuscript. Thanks go to Alicja Muszynski, Murray Knuttila and Claire Culhane for offering their support when it was most needed. We must also thank those fighting wrongful convictions from the trenches, particularly Tami Morrisroe and Thomas Sophonow.

Thanks also to Doug Smith for his valuable editing. Many people at Fernwood Publishing played a major role in making this book a reality. Errol Sharpe offered initial encouragement to write the book and pointed us in the right direction. Beverley Rach did an excellent job of laying out the pages and designing the cover. Donna Davis was a meticulous proof reader and caught many of our grammatical indiscretions. We would like to thank Wayne Antony of Fernwood Publishing for his tireless efforts in bringing this project to fruition. Without his assistance it simply would not have happened.

1

Introduction

THE SOCIAL REALITY OF WRONGFUL CONVICTION

Looking at them, the casual observer would see nothing unusual about the men seated in front of an audience in the conference room of a downtown Toronto hotel in May 1995. They might have been business people, politicians or academics. But David Milgaard, Donald Marshall and Guy Paul Morin were in fact men who had been wrongfully convicted of serious crimes. Milgaard served twenty-three years behind bars, Marshall served eleven years. Milgaard, Marshall and Morin have become public figures, symbols of a justice system gone wrong. After years of being ignored their cases had been championed by the media. They were household names. Many of them owed their freedom to the dedication of long-suffering family members who had pursued their cases for decades. Had they trusted in the justice system to identify and correct its own mistakes they would still be in prison. Their presence at this national convention of the Association in Defence of the Wrongly Convicted, indeed the fact that such an organization is needed, raises troubling questions about the Canadian justice system. How many more innocent Canadians are locked behind prison bars? Can we blame their convictions on simple human error or are there deeper problems in the Canadian justice system?

HOW MANY ARE WRONGFULLY CONVICTED?

There are many guilty people in prisons who insist they are innocent, hoping their claim will earn them their freedom. Unfortunately, there is no simple method for separating legitimate claims of innocence from those of the guilty or for determining the actual number of wrongfully convicted. In Canada very little research has been done in this area. The answer to the question of how many people are wrongfully convicted is therefore unknown and unknowable. We know only of cases that go to trial. As we will discuss later there may be thousands of cases of wrongful conviction in Canada because, for a variety of reasons, innocent people may plead guilty during plea bargaining. Although justice officials stress that wrongful convictions are rare occurrences, the available evidence indicates that the cases that do come to our attention are only the tip of the proverbial iceberg. In 1997, 690 Canadian convicts applied to the Canadian Government's Conviction Review Group (CRG). The CRG had only five staff members to review these cases (*Winnipeg Free Press*: August 21, 1997).

A study conducted at Long Lartin maximum security prison for the National Association of Parole Officers in Britain revealed that as many as 6 percent of the inmates of that prison may be wrongfully convicted. The association believed this figure was typical of other British prisons (Carvel 1992). British inmates who proclaim their innocence all said they face enormous difficulties trying to get the judicial system to listen to their complaints. As in Canada, British prisoners who protest their innocence also find it much more difficult to gain parole. Harry Fletcher, who headed the study, noted that

> many of the men have been trying to put together a case for up to ten years. All have experienced problems in getting adequate legal advice and some have been forced to draft their own appeal grounds, with no real hope of an adequate hearing. (Carvel 1992)

Only a few very committed lawyers were prepared to take on the tedious and time-consuming task of proving a miscarriage of justice with little prospect of any monetary reward.

A recent British Royal Commission report states that 700 to 800 cases of possible wrongful conviction are still waiting for review. The report also states that one-third of Britain's Police Departments are being investigated in connection with such cases. American criminologists Ronald Huff, Arye Rattner and Edward Sagarin (1986) reported that top justice officials in the United States believed that between 1 percent and 5 percent of all felony convictions were wrongful. In numerical terms, 1 percent translates into 6,000 cases per year. Hugo Bedau and Michael Radelet (1987), in researching wrongful convictions, concluded that twenty-three innocent persons have been executed in the United States between 1905 and 1974. Edwin Borchard, in his classic 1932 book, *Convicting the Innocent*, discussed sixty known American cases of wrongful conviction.

More recently, a Gannett News Service analysis found eighty-five instances over the past twenty years in which American prosecutors used fabricated or questionable evidence to convict innocent people (*USA Today* 1994).

Have Canadians bought the official message that there are too few wrongful convictions to be concerned about, that human error is bound to occur and that in any event the justice system will self-correct? Do we naively assume that a democratic political system automatically guarantees us a fair and equitable system of justice, free of corruption and political intrigue? Has our search for truth and justice been allowed to regress into a vilification of the innocent? Have we let our guard down and permitted race and class distinctions, political corruption and professional self-interests to pervade our justice system? These are unpleasant questions for which there are no immediate answers. Yet, as we will see, questions like these must, in part, guide our investigation into the cause of wrongful convictions.

THE OFFICIAL EXPLANATION

When a wrongful conviction is exposed police, judges, bureaucrats and politicians who bear responsibility for the design and maintenance of the system are quick to offer a ready explanation for why the system failed. This explanation is frequently echoed by academics in contemporary criminological literature. Miscarriages of justice are said to result primarily from poor witness reporting or by "unintended" errors committed by justice officials. Huff, Rattner and Sagarin (1996) note that most of the wrongful convictions they examined were the product of unintentional errors made by witnesses or by those who operate the American justice system. While Rattner (1983) indicates that many factors are involved in wrongful convictions, he notes that fully 52 percent of the cases he studied involved poor witness identification. Borchard (1932) emphasized the major role that witnesses can play in the wrongful conviction of the innocent. Jerome and Barbara Frank (1957) argue that a witness who gives false testimony frequently believes he or she is telling the truth. More recently, Philip Rosen (1992) noted the importance of bad eyewitness reporting as a causal factor in Canadian wrongful convictions. The true extent of the problems generated by eyewitness reporting can be seen in a recent *Globe and Mail* article (1995) which reported that a review of 1000 American wrongful convictions found that half of these were due to eyewitness errors. The same report found that each year nearly 80,000 trials in the United States rely on eyewitness testimony (*Globe and Mail*: January 21, 1995).

Eyewitness reporting is crucial to any comprehension of wrongful conviction. A key witness to a crime is sometimes the only evidence the prosecution has to make its case. Without the testimony of a witness to the event the prosecution may be forced to rely on circumstantial evidence, which most juries would find insufficient to bring down a verdict of guilty. An eyewitness to an event is a powerful weapon in the hands of the prosecution. History has shown that juries are inclined to accept the testimonies of witnesses as fact because they find it difficult to believe that people lie under oath. The end result is that tenuous eyewitness evidence becomes socially transformed into "fact."

Obviously, the official explanation of unavoidable human error as a prime cause of wrongful conviction cannot be discounted. Lawyers can be misinformed, witnesses may honestly believe they have seen something that they have not, judges may unconsciously give bad instructions to juries. People do make mistakes and that fact must be recognized. What we are suggesting here is that many of the official explanations for wrongful conviction miss the mark. The cases that we examine in this book demonstrate a consistent pattern of who becomes the victim and how they have been victimized. The official explanations ignore the fact that the underprivileged are most frequently the victims of this "human error."

At the most fundamental level we must surely consider the possibility that those with wealth can retain the best of defence counsels who will ensure that such "human error" does not often happen to them. When David Milgaard, Thomas Sophonow and Guy Paul Morin were finally able to attract high calibre lawyers to work on their cases, "human error" was "discovered" by the courts and their convictions were overturned. Furthermore, when a wrongful conviction is exposed and corrected, it is presented as evidence by the authorities that the system does work and is self-correcting. Ontario prosecutor Leo McGuigan put Guy Paul Morin behind bars for murder in 1993. When Morin was later proven innocent through DNA analysis, McGuigan told the press gathered outside the courthouse that "the justice system in this country is run by human beings. It does on occasion make mistakes. This was one of them" (Clayton 1995: 9). This audacious statement, from a man who only two years before had presented Morin to the jury as a sadistic mad killer, is typical of how those within the system rationalize wrongful convictions to the public. Overly-simplistic references to "unfortunate human error" do not capture the true nature of the unjust convictions studied in this book.

If we are to gain a comprehensive understanding of this phenomenon we must subject our justice system to two levels of analysis. The first, "on-the-ground" level involves the "hands-on" work of the professionals and bureaucrats who run the legal and justice systems. Their actions are the immediate cause of all convictions, wrongful and otherwise. The second and higher level of analysis involves an understanding of how the systemic political, economic and social inequality endemic to Canadian society leads to the marginalization of large groups of Canadians, some of whom become wrongfully convicted. The two levels are interdependent because bureaucratic and professional malfeasance generally occurs within the overarching context of social inequality and its commensurate marginalization of certain groups of peoples.

BUREAUCRATIC AND PROFESSIONAL WRONG-DOING

This on-the-ground level of analysis examines the targeting practices of the police, the suppression of evidence, police coercion and intimidation, falsified forensic evidence, judicial malpractice, jury tampering and prosecution and defence misconduct. Clayton (1995) contends that the most frequent causes of wrongful convictions in Britain include confessions obtained under pressure in the absence of a lawyer, fabrication of evidence, lack of forensic corroboration, untested alibis, unreliable prosecution witness, poor representation by defence lawyers and biased direction to the jury by judges.

Some American studies emphasize the role of eyewitness identification as a factor in wrongful convictions while still noting the importance of Clayton's findings. Rattner (1983, 1988) found 52 percent of all wrongful convictions studied involved eyewitness misidentification; 11 percent, perjury by witnesses; 10 percent, the negligence of criminal justice officials; 8 percent, coerced confessions by the police; 4 percent, a "frame-up"; and 3 percent, perjury by criminal justice officials. Other factors involved identification by police due to prior criminal record, forensic errors and "pure error" (Rattner 1983, 1988). Rattner (1983) also discovered that organizational and societal factors play a major role in wrongful conviction and that all levels of the criminal justice system tend to ratify earlier errors. Indeed, Rattner (1983) noted that the higher a case moved in the system, the less chance there was for an error to be recognized and corrected. This would seem to suggest that those at the highest level of judicial review close ranks and act as gatekeepers, thus protecting the integrity and public perception of the system.

Because they are particularly sensitive to public pressure, it is in the police's interest to solve a case quickly. Under these circumstances the police may target for arrest the first individual who has even the remotest chance of being involved in the crime. Convinced of the suspect's guilt, they feel justified in using any legal as well as illegal means, such as threats, brutality, perjury and suppression of evidence, to build a case against this person (Huff et al. 1996). If this unfortunate individual has a previous criminal record, comes from a visible minority and is already living on the fringes of society, he or she will have few resources with which to defend him- or herself against police power and public indifference.

Adding to the problem is the fact that the police feel that they do society's "dirty work" but receive no recognition for a job well done. All this culminates in a "we against them" mentality and a tendency for the police to be secretive in their actions and suspicious of the public. This suspicion, directed primarily against those of the lower class, is one of the key factors leading to police coercion and brutality and the targeting of the poor that is endemic to wrongful convictions. Also, because promotion within police ranks is determined in part by an officer's clean record and the number of high profile arrests and cases completed, an officer will be tempted into wrongdoing in order to secure a conviction. All this represents an organizational culture and structure in which winnable (and won) cases are a priority and become a self-maintaining process. Under these circumstances an innocent suspect is well on the way to a wrongful conviction. We will see later how Donald Marshall Jr., a Nova Scotia Mi'kmaw, was quickly singled out by the Sydney police as a prime murder suspect. Guy Paul Morin was targeted as a prime murder suspect because he was considered "weird" by an Ontario regional police department. David Milgaard, a sixteen-year-old high-school drop-out and self-professed hippie became the prime suspect of a conservative Saskatoon police force headed by a chief who made it known that he had no use for hippies. All of these men, and others to be discussed in the case chapters, were marginalized in one way or another from mainstream middle-class society.

In this book we demonstrate that the police, in building their case against a prime suspect, may suppress, lose, misinterpret or overlook evidence that supports the defendant's claim of innocence. Once the police have convinced themselves that they have apprehended the guilty person, they proceed on the assumption that the accused and any witnesses whose evidence supports the accused's claims of innocence are lying. On the other hand, any evidence that appears to point to the defendant's guilt may be exaggerated out of all proportion. Furthermore, evidence or testimony that points to alternative suspects may be repressed or totally ignored. This form of police misconduct is much less likely to be detected or challenged if it is perpetrated against the powerless members of society rather than the middle and upper classes.

Another aspect of professional wrong-doing involves what is frequently referred to as "jailhouse testimony." Jailhouse confessions involve an alleged confession of guilt by an accused to a fellow inmate who has been planted in a cell by the prosecution or police. The "plant" later testifies in court that the accused confessed to the crime. In exchange for this testimony the witness may be given special consideration by the police or the prosecution. The fact that the accused in this instance may have been "set up" and that a deal was made with the planted inmate may not be known by the judge, the jury the accused's lawyer or the public.

Coerced eyewitness testimony is also an example of professional misconduct on the part of the judicial authorities. Testimony gained through coercion may be presented by a variety of people, including the friends and family of both the accused and the victim. These people will swear in court that they saw the accused at the scene of the crime or even commit the criminal act. Unfortunately, the process of coercion is made relatively simple if the witness already harbours racial or class-based attitudes concerning the accused that blurs the distinction between truth and falsification. The police may also easily coerce a witness into giving false testimony against an accused if the witness expects to gain some favour by co-operating with the police. This is frequently the motivation of the typical "jailbird confessor. Many witnesses to a violent crime may have gotten only a fleeting look at their attacker and are initially reluctant to identify a possible suspect from a police line-up or mug book. These witnesses may be encouraged or coached by the police to identify a person as being the one they saw at the scene of the crime.

Expert witnesses for the prosecution, such as forensic scientists, may step over the boundaries separating science from advocacy. We will see later how forensic scientists have misrepresented the results of laboratory findings in a manner prejudicial to the accused but favourable to the prosecution's case. It is also possible for forensic scientists to repress forensic evidence that would be beneficial to the accused.

We must also consider the possibility of biased judges. These individuals are at the pinnacle of the judicial system and their job is to oversee the trial process and determine the sentence for those convicted of a crime. It is the responsibility of the judge to guarantee that all parties involved in a trial act according to the proscribed rules, assuring a fair and impartial hearing for the accused. Judges therefore have a tremendous responsibility to maintain justice. However, they also have the very important task of maintaining public confidence in the judicial system and emphasizing its legitimacy. To this end, lawyer Alastair Logan (1995) asserts, the judiciary will act to preserve the reputations of police officers, prosecutors, expert witnesses or others acting on behalf of the Crown when their reputation or the system is called into question. The possibility therefore exists that a judge may unintentionally or maliciously conduct a trial or instruct the jury in a way that is prejudicial to the accused, if he or she perceives that to do otherwise would somehow jeopardize the integrity of the judicial system.

We must recognize that prosecution and defence misconduct may lead to a wrongful conviction. The Canadian system of justice is based on an adversarial process that pits the formidable forces of the state against a lone individual. In theory, the power of the state should be nullified by the skill of the defence lawyer as he or she does courtroom battle with the prosecutor. This adversarial system demands a winner and a loser but, unfortunately, the reasons for winning go beyond simply seeing justice done. Winning for lawyers becomes a means of building a reputation, of earning more money, of living a good life. Those lawyers who have mastered the techniques of examination, cross-examination and other courtroom mysteries will naturally be rewarded with a higher income and the respect of their peers. Unfortunately, the desire to win has caused many lawyers to engage in questionable, even unscrupulous, tactics, which are frequently condoned by the legal profession as a whole. Lawyers learn quickly what works well in the courtroom and what does not. What works are techniques that may distort the truth, confuse the jury and make apparent liars out of honest witnesses. The legal system is highly structured and those within it share a culture that emphasizes winning cases rather than doing justice. For too many lawyers the courtroom has become a place for winning cases and building reputations rather than a forum for discovering truth and serving justice. When the need to win takes precedent over truth, the seeds of wrongful conviction have been sown in the fertile soil of legal indifference, personal greed and public apathy.

The antithesis to the overly combative lawyers for whom winning is the ultimate goal is the defence counsel who does not defend. Forty-four-year-old Wilbert Coffin was hanged in 1956 for the murder of three American bear hunters. Many people now believe he did not commit the crime. In a book on the Coffin case, the late Jacques Hebert argued that the incompetent performance of Coffin's lawyer contributed to Coffin's conviction and subsequent execution. The legal counsel for Donald Marshall Jr. is regarded by many as having been ineffective. Most lawyers are skilled and responsible professionals dedicated to insuring the propriety of the legal system in all its ramifications. That even a few should deviate from this ideal casts a dark shadow over the entire system and frequently leads to convicting the innocent. When asked to defend a client who is obviously not guilty, the legal-aid lawyer may not have the financial and human resources needed to provide the appropriate defence for the accused against an aggressive and determined prosecutor with the resources of the state at hand.

The bureaucratic and professional wrong-doing described above does not happen in isolation from the mainstream of society. Such behaviour has its source in the systemic social inequality endemic in the Canadian social structure. The analysis of wrongful conviction must therefore focus on the social structure itself—on Canadian society—and it is here that we must now turn our attention.

Social Inequality, Crime and Wrongful Conviction

Canada, like other western industrialized nations, is a country characterized by systematic social inequality. Vast differences in life chances between classes and racial groups are clearly evident. Most telling is the high and persistent poverty in Canada. From the 1970s to the 1990s between 15 percent and 18 percent of Canadians are classified as poor by the federal government. In fact, by Statistics Canada's estimation, which many argue seriously understates the problem, over five million Canadians, 17.8 percent of our population, were poor in 1995 (Ross and Shillington 1989: 40; Battle 1998). Moreover, in recent decades it seems the rich are getting richer. Between the 1970s and 1990s the share of national income going to the bottom 50 percent of the population dropped from almost 28 percent to under 23 percent while the top 10 percent saw their income increase by almost 14 percent (Yalnizyan 1994: 22). Aboriginal people in Canada are in even worse conditions: in 1991, for example, the average income for Aboriginal people was $14,561 compared to $24,001 for all Canadians. Similarly, in 1991, almost half of Aboriginals had incomes of under $10,000, more than twice that for all Canadians (Battle 1997). It is in this context that we must view the operation of our criminal justice system.

Justice is essentially an abstract concept based on the rather vague ideas that people share about law and society, crime and punishment, good and bad, and justice will change as society itself changes. Many of these ideas, including our laws, become institutionalized and regarded as natural truths—the very foundation of society itself. Once institutionalized, these laws become a powerful tool for maintaining the legitimacy of the social order by deflecting public attention away from those state agencies and institutions that may be wrong or illegal, and towards individual wrongdoers, emphasizing the fact that the activities of such people are detrimental to the stability of social order itself. Unfortunately the majority of those singled out by the judicial system as being the most undesirable and dangerous wrong-doers are the poor, the unemployed and the visible minorities living on the fringes of society. These unfortunate people, frequently underprivileged since birth, thus become our criminals. Structured as it is, the judicial system permits select people with authority to pass judgment on others in a process that will officially certify them as criminal. In practice, the legal system becomes not

17

only an extension of the social values and attitudes of a society at any particular point in time but also a powerful weapon used by the state to control the dispossessed groups, particularly during times of political and social upheaval (Bonger 1967; Scott and Skull 1978).

Scholars in both critical and mainstream criminology have extensively documented the fact that criminal law is not applied equally to all classes in society. This leads to the lower class being certified as the criminal class (Hogarth 1971; Mandel 1991; Reiman 1990; Myers 1991; Maclean 1986; Tepperman 1977; Bell-Rowbotham and Boydell 1972). These researchers tell us that the lower class is convicted more frequently than the upper class because the ideology as well as the actions of the police and others in the justice system weeds out and protects higher status offenders from prosecution for the types of crimes that most frequently draw the attention of the police. It is the poor, the unemployed, the visible minorities, the powerless and those ostracized for their sexual orientation who are most frequently criminalized by the system. These groups from the lower class most properly fit our definition of marginalized peoples. However, under some circumstances, a person from other than the lower class may also be considered marginalized because he or she is different from the social norm. Guy Paul Morin was middle-class, but he was also marginalized because his lifestyle was not acceptable to his community. When the police questioned him they considered him "weird."

To complicate the problem, many marginalized people are sensitive to the fact that what does and does not become defined as "criminal" may work against them. As a result of this understanding that the law and its application are frequently biased, insulting and injurious towards them, the marginalized may behave in ways that bring them into direct conflict with the law. This is a classic example of the self-fulfilling prophecy.

In the United States the corrections system handles about 1.3 million offenders per day. Eighty percent of the people in this group comes from the lowest 15 percent income group. Looked at another way, of the approximately one-half million people in state prisons in 1986, 30 percent were not employed and 42 percent were without full-time employment prior to their arrest (Myers 1991; Reiman 1990). Beverley Bell-Rowbotham and Craig Boydell (1972) found that the highest rates of conviction in Canada were for people with little or no schooling and low-status occupations, with labourers having the highest rate. Lorne Tepperman (1977) noted that the police, prosecutors, judges and probation officers working within the Canadian justice system have been given a great deal of discretion in carrying out their duties towards the accused. Whenever this discretion is available it will be used in ways detrimental to the poor. William Chambliss and Robert Siedman (1971) agree with Tepperman, arguing that this discretion will be utilized by the legal and judicial authorities to bring the poor and powerless into the purview of the law. As a result, the laws prohibiting certain types of behaviour popular among the lower class are the most likely to be enforced.

Lower-status offenders are also less likely to be granted bail or recommendations for leniency from probation officers and others within the system. Accused persons who are not granted bail face severe problems. First of all they are kept in jail, as if they had already been convicted. While in jail an accused person cannot seek out witnesses and evidence that could help in their defence. Studies have shown that those released on bail while awaiting trial are more likely to be acquitted or receive lighter sentences than those who are incarcerated while awaiting trial (Ares et al. 1963; Friedland 1965).

Even where crimes are identical, the courts will frequently give a middle- or upper-class offender a lighter sentence than that given a lower-class offender. It is assumed and sometimes stated by the court that since the upper-class offender has already "suffered enough" through loss of status brought about by the arrest and trial, incarceration would be socially and psychologically destructive. There is no empirical evidence to support this prejudicial notion that the poor suffer less than the rich from the humiliation and degradation of prison. Michael Mandel suggests, " [T]he tender attitude displayed to high status offenders by sentencing judges merely betrays their sympathy for the problems associated with their own class and their insensitivity to those of the working and marginal classes" (1991: 152).

Jeffrey Reiman, (1990) notes that weeding out the wealthy from the criminal certification process starts with the police deciding who to investigate, arrest and charge. The decision is not made simply on the basis of the offense committed, but also through a systematic class bias that works against the poor. This weeding process on the part of the police, combined with the class sympathies of the judiciary, cause our jails and penitentiaries to be populated predominantly by those from the fringes of society.

Afro-Canadian and First Nations people in particular seem to be targeted by the system for arrest, conviction and punishment. When a member of a visible minority is murdered the criminal justice system does not give the case high priority, but the killing of a white person by a member of a visible minority will cause the justice system to act with the greatest urgency (Radelet et al. 1986). Although Canada's Aboriginal people represent only about 2 percent of the total population, they constitute 10 percent of the population of Canada's federal prisons. In the prairies, where the Native population is about 5 percent of the total, 32 percent of the inmate population is Native. More specifically, in Saskatchewan and Manitoba, Aboriginal people represents 6 percent to 7 percent of the total population but 46 percent to 60 percent of the prison inmates (Stephens 1991).

Crime is also an economic engine for society. It generates employment for the police, lawyers, judges, court officials, prison guards and all the ancillary agencies that work within and support the system. Even the state-funded legal-defence systems, designed to close the obvious gap in the quality of justice between the classes has met with only limited success. The poor still get young, overworked and inexperienced lawyers who have little time to prepare an adequate defence for their clients. These systems seem to benefit the legal profession by creating a new source of guaranteed income while legitimizing the state (Snider 1985).

In the same vein, Friedenberg, commenting on the legal industry notes:

> it all rests on the backs of about 25,000 poor—mostly very poor—souls in jail. Most of them are less than thirty years old and have never finished school; a disproportionate number of them are Native people. In what other way could these few—these gallant if not happy few—impoverished in body and mind and often in spirit, contribute so much to their country? (1980: 283)

Justice is essentially a system of social control. Historically it has favoured the interests of the powerful who have determined the law's content and implementation. A state that acts on behalf of the ruling class determines the laws, who will be certified as criminal and what punishments will be levied (Panitch 1977). The majority of those caught and convicted for criminal activities have consistently been from the ranks of the disadvantaged. For any given crime the poor are more likely to be arrested; if arrested, to be charged; if charged, more likely to be convicted; if convicted, more likely to be sent to prison; and if sent to prison, more likely to receive a longer term than deviants from other classes (Reiman 1990). The explanation for these disproportionate conviction rates among Canada's marginalized population will not simply be found in the behaviour of the poor, but in the class and racial biases infesting our society. But what has this bias, which leads to the conviction and punishment of the poor, got to do with wrongful convictions?

If arrest, conviction and the type of sentence are biased against the poor and the minorities in our society, is it not logical to assume that wrongful conviction will be shaped by the same social forces? Our society is fraught with serious structural inequalities based on class and race which frequently transforms the Western ideal of justice into a utilitarian search for a conviction. As revealed in several studies carried out in Britain and the United States, this search for a conviction all too often ends with a marginalized individual becoming the victim of a miscarriage of justice (Carvel 1992; Huff et al. 1986; Bedau and Radelet 1987). Often poor, uneducated and powerless, these wrongly accused end up incarcerated or executed for a crime they did not commit.

Even factors as seemingly innocuous as eyewitness reporting of a crime may be jaundiced by social inequality. It is unfortunate that we do not have more scientific information regarding the major causes of wrongful eyewitness reporting in criminal trials. We should, however, be conscious of the fact that eyewitnesses themselves are frequently marginalized people who are easily coerced by the police and prosecution. Faulty eyewitness evidence led to the initial convictions of Donald Marshall Jr., David Milgaard and Thomas Sophonow. As the following chapters demonstrate, the faulty testimony was not simply the result of human error. The witnesses were pressured by police to the point where they abandoned their original testimony and presented false evidence. Witnesses are not immune to the socially structured prejudice, discrimination, racism and bigotry that characterizes our society. The notion that because eyewitness give evidence under oath they are somehow free of prejudice and bigotry plays into the hands of the apologists who would have us believe that wrongful convictions are a product of chance error.

Eyewitnesses are influenced, consciously or unconsciously, by their personal notions of truth and reality. Thus an eyewitness who harbours a fear or hatred of a particular minority or racial group may incorrectly think the suspect they saw at the scene of the crime was a member of that group, but in reality the suspect was not. Ideological beliefs do influence our perceptions of reality, including what and who we may have seen at any given point in time. And as long as such ideologies and attitudes are sustained by the social structure, eyewitness reporting must be considered suspect.

Because the police play such a dominant role in wrongful convictions it is important to understand that their malevolent actions frequently find their genesis in the social inequality characteristic of Canadian society. It was noted above how police activity concentrates on the marginalized groups in society and has stereotyped them as criminal (Reiman 1990). This false stereotype discriminates and ignores individual differences among marginalized peoples. This pre-judging by the police leads to increased surveillance, harassment, arrest and conviction of members of these groups. This will almost guarantee that those who are wrongfully convicted in society will predominantly come from the marginalized sectors.

It is no longer acceptable to suggest that wrongful conviction resulting from police activities is simply the result of numerous bizarre elements coincidentally coming together. Wrongful convictions are frequently the result of the mundane and malevolent behaviour of various state agents, including the police, which is being directed against minority groups and marginalized peoples. This is not to suggest that the police are ideologically unique in their attitudes towards marginalized groups. They simply reflect the values and culture of which they are part. Indeed, R.H.D. Head, the Assistant Commissioner of the Royal Canadian Mounted Police has stated "We have a racial intolerance within the force because, as a product of a larger Canadian society we enter its ranks with all the usual bias, prejudice and racism baggage that this society generates" (quoted in Harding 1991: 363–383).

Regardless of this bold confession, police officers who have targeted the underprivileged will deny this activity to protect themselves from loss of promotion, loss of job and criminal charges. People who have been harassed or intimidated by the police must make their case against police officers who are generally regarded by the public and members of juries as stalwart, respectable defenders of the law. Marginalized individuals are frequently regarded with suspicion or fear by a predominantly white, middle-class population. Their charges against the police are unlikely to be given serious consideration. Such public apathy plays a major role in the outcome of any investigation of police misconduct (Anderson and Winfree 1987).

Lawyers, judges and juries are also major players in the drama of wrongful convictions. Their actions are often rooted in an inequitable social structure. Marginalized peoples do not have the economic means to pay for top-level legal counsel. They must rely on young, inexperienced, underpaid and overworked legal-aid lawyers to defend them. These people have neither the time or the resources to mount a good defence for their client. This leads the poor to becoming the classic victims of plea-bargaining pressure. Reiman (1990), notes that the vast majority of criminal convictions in the United States are concluded through plea bargaining. In Canada, R.V. Ericson and P.M. Baranek (1982) found that over half the lawyers they interviewed admitted to plea bargaining. The police were frequently involved in these discussions. Many of those lawyers who plea bargained felt that the bargain they had reached brought no real advantage for the accused, since the police had overcharged their client in the first place. In the plea bargaining process people are often advised by their lawyers to plead guilty to crimes they did not commit to avoid going to trial for a greater charge.

Why do accused but innocent people agree to plea bargain their case? For one thing, these individuals may know that there is considerable circumstantial evidence against them, and that the probability of being found guilty and sentenced to a long prison term or death is high. They may feel, correctly or incorrectly, that they have little choice but to bargain with the prosecution for a lesser charge and sentence in exchange for their guilty plea. There is also the possibility of legal pressure being put on the accused to plea bargain. If, for example, the suspect is not a model citizen, has a criminal record, is of the lower class or comes from a visible minority, there is a strong possibility he or she will be represented by an overworked and underpaid legal-aid lawyer who will encourage them to make a deal with the prosecution so they can get on with their next case (Huff et al. 1996). Even if the defence lawyer is not from legal aid, a plea bargain may be encouraged because a lawyer will benefit financially by concluding as many cases as possible in the shortest period of time. Likewise, prosecutors and others in a cash-strapped justice system are anxious to move cases through the system as quickly as possible. There exists an unspoken agreement among defence counsel, prosecutors, judges and others within the system to encourage the defendant to plead guilty (Hagan 1977). During these pre-trial negotiations, which occur behind closed doors, judicial control and rules of evidence are not available to the accused (Tepperman 1977). The accused pleads guilty and does not protest his or her innocence. As a result the miscarriage of justice goes undetected. Plea bargaining is a cheap and efficient method of dispensing justice, one which can lead to poor people being wrongfully convicted.

Prosecuting lawyers are vulnerable to charges of professional misconduct leading to wrongful conviction. A trial is an adversarial tournament between jousting lawyers played out before a judge and jury. Theoretically the Crown prosecutor's paramount responsibility is to ensure that justice is done. If the prosecutor becomes aware of information that casts serious doubt on the guilt of the accused, the prosecutor is supposed to share such information with the court. If necessary, the Crown should drop all charges. Unfortunately, this does not always happen.

The Crown prosecutor has access to state funding, police services and forensic expertise. Counsel for the defence may be significantly hampered by the accused's inability to pay for services. The prosecution's discretionary privileges include the right to reduce a charge from the more serious to less serious, reduce the number of charges outstanding against the accused, order a stay of proceedings or entirely withdraw the charges. Unfortunately, in many instances the discretion exercised by the prosecution is not carried out in the interest of justice but may be informed by the prosecutor's own attitude about the accused, the profile level of the case and the political and personal implications of winning or losing (Tepperman 1977). While the majority of lawyers regard themselves as respectable middle-class professionals serving a necessary function in society, they are also individuals who have deeply ingrained middle-class views and values about crime and criminals. One may logically expect that prosecutors and defenders will be inclined to first serve their own class-biased interests before dedicating their services to those on the fringes of society. Some lawyers have a profound understanding of the true nature of social injustice and dedicate their lives to serving the underprivileged, but they are a rare breed. Lacking the services of the most skilled of lawyers, those of the lower classes more quickly fall victim to the injustice of justice.

Because judges as a group are near the top of the social structure does not mean that they are isolated from the racism, classism, politics and other biasing realities of our society. Judges have a value system that shapes their worldview and the way in which they approach their work. John Hogarth (1971) notes that judges as a group have a perception of themselves as being in and of the Canadian elite. They are well-educated, prosperous, conservative and similar to the police in their intolerance for deviants and their belief in the efficacy of penal servitude. In 1974 the Law Reform Commission of Canada noted that the treatment of accused individuals by judges reflects the concern of any prosperous person for life and property when dealing with the poor. Aware of their privileged social position, judges are not about to advocate changes to the system that is the source of their power. As a general rule, the public, including those serving as jury members, are unaware of potential judicial bias. As a result they regard judges as wise and impartial adjudicators concerned only with seeing justice served. This public attitude toward the judiciary gives judges the social and legal ability to greatly influence any decision rendered by a jury.

Forensic experts frequently work closely with the police, prosecutors and Crown lawyers. The evidence presented in court by these scientists determines the outcome of many trials. These specialists take pride in telling us that forensic evidence is not tainted by the subjectivity that can plague social science research and the law. It is true that the tremendous advances made in forensics in recent years has caused much of the scientific evidence presented in court to be accepted as virtual truth. Unfortunately, while the science itself may be highly objective, the same cannot be said for all the scientists. Barry Tarlow (1995) cites numerous cases of evidence tampering by forensic experts, who were acting on behalf of the prosecution. For example, Fred Zain was Chief Physical Evidence Officer of Bexar County, Texas from 1989 to 1993. During this time he "systematically falsified, misinterpreted and exaggerated forensic tests and results which may have lead to the conviction of hundreds of individuals" (Tarlow 1995: 18). In San Francisco, as many as one thousand people may have been convicted of drug-related offenses over the past five years because a police department chemist falsified drug tests and results (Tarlow 1995). We will see later how Stephanie Nyznyk, a laboratory technician working out of the Centre for Forensic Sciences in Ontario, suppressed the fact that hair and fibre samples used by the prosecution to successfully convict Guy Paul Morin of murder had been contaminated and should have been discarded as evidence.

The British and American research noted above proves beyond any reasonable doubt that serious miscarriages of justice resulting in wrongful convictions are not isolated events. The only evidence we have emerges from the more sensational crimes that generate media attention, primarily murder. Unfortunately, the factors of powerlessness and inequality that are the root cause of wrongful convictions in the first place are also the factors preventing the wrongfully convicted from establishing their innocence. Proving one is wrongfully convicted requires money, but it also requires many middle-class social attributes and skills unfamiliar to marginalized people. Consequently, for most of the wrongfully convicted, it is a classic case of "out of sight, out of mind" and only the most fortunate among them will gain their freedom.

The Canadian justice system is class-based. Laws are made by middle-class politicians for middle-class people, enforced by middle-class police, argued over by middle-class lawyers and arbitrated by middle-class judges who sentence mostly lower-class people to prisons run by middle-class administrators. At no point do marginalized people play a role in developing or administrating the system. Excluded from the mainstream, they are frequently swept up in the net of social injustice by the very institution that should protect them. The systemic inequalities ensure that the marginalized will be the criminals and the wrongfully convicted.

The following six case reviews are only a sample of the many known instances of wrongful conviction in Canada. They should give the reader a deeper insight into the contributing factors leading to this unfortunate phenomenon. The cases presented here were purposely selected for several reasons. Some have received extensive media exposure, but this exposure, while long on description and sensationalism, has been short on analysis regarding the social forces that led to the convictions. The less well-known cases were selected, not because they supported a particular theoretical point of view, but because they are truly representative of the vast majority of wrongful convictions. Had space permitted, other cases such as those of William Nepoose, Eric Biddle, Tommy Ross and Patrick Kelly, as well as countless documented British and American cases, would have been included. These too would confirm what the cases presented here clearly show: the root cause of wrongful convictions is to be found primarily in the social structure itself, not in individual failings.

It is consistently denied by judges, lawyers, prosecutors and the police that politics, racism, sexism and professional interests influence their respective roles within the justice system. As the cases of Donald Marshall, Guy Paul Morin and others attest, this is a myth perpetrated on an unsuspecting public. Regardless of what those who control the justice system tell us, it is a fundamentally flawed system infected with overt secrecy, corruption, brutality, racism and class prejudice on the part of some police, lawyers, judges and others who work within the system. It is not surprising, therefore, that those who are wrongfully convicted are the marginalized of society, the direct victims of the systemic biases inherent in our social structure. As Radelet et al. (1986) note, the ideal that all people are born with an equal chance of dying in the electric chair is a myth. Alastair Logan says it best when he states that the racism that was so much a part of Donald Marshall's life "walked ahead of him into the police station, into his lawyer's office and into his court of trial. It directed the quality of justice he received" (1995:7).

2

The Case of
Donald Marshall

THE DEFENDANT

Except for the fact that his father was Grand Chief of the Mi'kmaq nation, Donald Marshall Jr. was not much different from the other five hundred people living on the Membertou reserve near Sydney, Nova Scotia. Like his peers, the good-looking seventeen-year-old was a product of the alcoholism, poor housing, high unemployment and petty crime that characterize Canada's reserve system. He and his young friends formed a street gang and were frequently in trouble with the law. Consequently Marshall was well known to the local police. He was big for his age and his reputation as a skilled street fighter earned him the respect of rival gangs and the admiration of his peers. Despite the fact that he was destined to become Grand Chief, an honourary position, Donald Marshall Jr. was nonetheless a man without a future. He had failed two grades in school and had been expelled from school when he was fifteen. Rejected and feared by much of the white population of Sydney, he was denied access to mainstream society and could look only inward to a life on the reserve. The fact that he was a Mi'kmaw living in a racist society assured that Donald Marshall Jr. was an angry young man on the margins of Canadian society.

THE CRIME

On the evening of May 28, 1971, Marshall and his friends set out, as they had often done in the past, for the weekend dance at St. Joseph's Parish Hall in Sydney. Sandy Seale, a young Afro-Canadian, also wanted to attend the dance, but when he found it was sold out he headed for Kings Road, intending to catch a bus home. On the way he met Marshall. They knew each other but were not close friends. Seale told Marshall (known as Junior to his friends) that the dance was sold out and that he was on his way home. Marshall asked Seale if he wanted to make some money. Seale asked him how they could do that. Marshall said they would bum the money from someone or just take it if necessary.[1] Panhandling and mugging were not activities with which Seale was familiar, but he did not oppose the idea.

Looking for victims the two youths strolled through Wentworth Park, crossed a footbridge and headed up the rise toward Crescent Street. It was here that they encountered Roy Newman Ebsary and James MacNeil. Of all the people which they could have met during their evening quest for easy money, few could have been more dangerous than Roy Ebsary.

MacNeil and Ebsary made an unusual pair. Ebsary was a tiny fifty-nine-year-old with a twisted and knotted goatee that matched his straggly white hair. MacNeil was an awkward, inarticulate twenty-five-year-old who seemed mesmerized by Ebsary's storytelling and his swashbuckling manner. Those who did not know Ebsary well viewed him as a simpleminded eccentric who draped a tattered blue Burberry over his shoulders and wore fake war medals on his chest. He spent much of his time frequenting the bars of Sydney regaling anyone who would listen with imaginary stories of his wartime naval exploits. He was fond of telling how he was decorated for his role in the sinking of the *Bismarck*. But as Donald Marshall Jr. and Sandy Seale were to discover, Roy Ebsary was not the harmless old alcoholic he appeared. There was an dark side to this aging little man that was soon to manifest itself in a violent rage that would take the life of Sandy Seale and rob Donald Marshall of his youth.

Marshall and Seale hinted to Ebsary and MacNeil that they were broke. Ebsary ignored the hint but invited the boys back to his place for a drink, an invitation they declined. The conversation was interrupted when two of Marshall's acquaintances, twenty-year-old Terry Gushue and fourteen-year-old Patricia Harriss, walked by. Gushue, who was quite drunk, asked Marshall for a light. Marshall left Seale with Ebsary and MacNeil and gave Gushue the light. When Harriss, intrigued by Ebsary's unusual appearance asked who the two men were, Marshall simply said, "They're crazy."

As Gushue and Harriss left, Marshall turned to find that Ebsary and MacNeil were also leaving. Marshall called them back, suggesting more forcefully that he and Seale wanted some money. Marshall grabbed MacNeil, who appeared to be the stronger of the two, in hopes that Ebsary would hand over some cash to Seale. This, as it turned out, was a fatal error in judgment. Ebsary had been mugged in the park several times before and had vowed that the next person who accosted him "would die in his tracks" (Harris 1986: 42; Barss Donham 1989: 54). In a matter of seconds Ebsary stabbed Seale in the stomach and slashed Marshall's arm. Seale slumped to the ground, his hands trying to cover the wound, while a terrified Marshall ran from the scene.

Marshall continued to run along Crescent Street until he overtook fourteen-year-old Maynard Chant who was hurrying along Byng Avenue toward George Street. Donald showed Chant his arm and told him Seale had been stabbed and was still in the park. Marshall and Chant caught a ride in a passing car and returned to the park where Chant tried to stop Seale's bleeding with his shirt. Chant and Marshall's conversation on Byng Avenue had been overheard by Marvel Mattson, a retired RCMP officer, through his open bedroom window. He telephoned the Sydney city police and told them something may have happened in the park. Before Marshall and Chant reached the park, Seale, still alive and in agony, had been discovered by a young couple who had left the dance. It was only when Marshall and Chant returned that the four young people rushed to a nearby house to call the police.

After the owner of the house assured them he would call the police, the four headed back to the scene but were intercepted by the police car responding to Mattson's call. Marshall described the attackers' appearance to the police and showed the constables his wound. The officers pushed Marshall into their car and sped to the crime scene. By the time they arrived, a second squad car was already there, along with a sizable crowd of onlookers. The Sydney police were relatively inexperienced with violent crime and the officers were shocked at the spectacle of Seale's intestines oozing out on to the pavement. This inexperience showed when the police neglected to have one of their members ride to the hospital in the ambulance with Seale. Had they done so Seale may have been able to provide them with valuable information about his attackers. By the time he arrived at the hospital Seale had lost most of his blood and was near death.

Meanwhile, Maynard Chant had been all but forgotten in the excitement. He had recovered his bloody shirt from the scene but was still faced with the problem of finding a ride back to Louisbourg. He had made his way to George Street hoping to hitch a ride home when a police car pulled up beside him and stopped. Staring at the bloody shirt in Chant's hand, the concerned officer wanted to know what had happened. "Do you know about the stabbing in the park?" Chant asked. In answer, the officer asked Chant if he had seen anything. "Yeah, I seen it all," lied Chant (Barss Donham 1989: 177). The officers then took Chant to the hospital.

We may never know if Chant's admissions were simply thoughtless words uttered by a tired and excited young man or an attempt to gain some sense of personal importance. Whatever the reason, the lie was to play a major part in the subsequent prosecution and conviction of Donald Marshall Jr. for the murder of Sandy Seale.

THE INVESTIGATION

Detective Michael MacDonald was off duty and at home when he received a call about the Seale stabbing. He rushed to the hospital but the doctor would not allow him to question the dying man. He then interviewed Donald Marshall Jr., who was at the hospital and had indicated a willingness to help the police in any way. Marshall described the assailants to MacDonald, although he did not tell him about the failed robbery. Unfortunately, the police handling of this case from the very first evening was inept. MacDonald, for reasons known only to him, did not take a formal statement from Marshall or Chant at the hospital nor did he bother to circulate a description of the assailants to other members of the Sydney police force. Furthermore, the scene of the crime was neither secured or searched, the names of people in the park at the time of the crime were not recorded and people in the neighbourhood were not questioned about anything unusual they may have seen that evening.

The man in charge of the investigation was Sergeant of Detectives John MacIntyre. He had several run-ins with Marshall in the past and the two men viewed each other with distrust. When he came on duty the morning after the incident, he reviewed the files of the investigating officers and summoned Donald Marshall for an interview. Marshall repeated his account of the incident but MacIntyre, like the officers before him, did not take a formal statement.

Sandy Seale died at 8:05 p.m. Saturday, May 29 without identifying his assailant. The Sydney police were now looking for a killer. Sydney's last homicide five years before had gone unsolved and the community would be in no mood for a repeat performance. The police were sensitive to this and to the demand that Seale's killer be quickly apprehended. The recently created Nova Scotia Black United Front issued at statement calling for a "quick and speedy apprehension of the assailant or assailants (Harris 1986: 67). It was imperative to MacIntyre that an arrest be made and the sooner the better. MacIntyre quickly formulated a theory that Marshall had killed Seale in the course of an argument. Before interviewing any witnesses or taking a formal statement from Marshall, MacIntyre sent a telex early on the morning of May 30 stating that "investigation to date reveals Marshall probably the person responsible" (Harris 1986: 63).

Remembering that Chant had said "I seen it all," MacIntyre and another officer drove to Louisbourg to question him further. MacIntyre questioned the boy in the police car in the absence of his parents and Chant repeated the story of the crime as it was related to him by Marshall: that two men had stabbed Marshall and Seale. He implied however, that he had seen the event, not just heard about it from Marshall. Chant was then taken to the Sydney police station where he gave a formal statement. Chant left the police station feeling that the police were not happy with his story, but he did not know what they wanted to hear from him.

Another police witness was John Pratico, a teenage acquaintance of Marshall. Someone had tipped the police that Pratico may have been an eyewitness to the killing, so MacIntyre called him in for questioning. Nervous and bewildered by the interrogation, Pratico at first denied any knowledge of the event. Indeed, all Pratico knew about the event was what he had heard on the radio and what Marshall had told him the day after the killing. But the police thought he knew something and pressured him until he slowly began to build a fictitious story that he hoped would please the police. His concocted description of what he saw involved two men running from the scene of the crime and jumping into a white Volkswagen. One of the men he described as being six-feet tall and dressed in a gray suit, the second man was five-and-a-half-feet tall and dressed in a brown corduroy jacket. He said he had seen all this while standing by the courthouse. MacIntyre now had signed eyewitnesses statements from Chant and Pratico describing the event they had seen in the park as well as the verbal description of Ebsary given to him by Marshall.

The problem was that all three witnesses were giving him different descriptions of the assailants.

MacIntyre returned to Wentworth Park at midnight and discovered that Pratico could not have seen the events if he had been standing by the courthouse. The youth was obviously lying and the next day MacIntyre confronted him with his lie and demanded the truth. Pratico again went to his original story that he had not really seen anything in the park. MacIntyre did not like this version and told Pratico that if he did not tell the truth he would be put in jail until he did. Pratico was taken back to the police station and questioned further by MacIntyre and Detective Sergeant William Urquhart. Pratico began to understand what it was the police wanted him to say. He told the officers that he was walking towards the tracks when he saw Seale and Marshall on the other side of the bridge arguing about something. He said he saw Marshall's left hand driving towards Seale's stomach and then pulling back. Seale fell to the ground and Marshall ran up Crescent Street towards Argyle Street. Pratico added that no one else was in the area at the time. MacIntyre had just heard an account of the crime from an eyewitness that supported his own suspicion that Donald Marshall Jr. was the killer of Sandy Seale. If he could extract a similar account of the event from Maynard Chant the case would be all but wrapped up.

MacIntyre and Urquhart arranged to talk to Chant and his mother in the Louisbourg Town Hall. "All we want is the truth from Chant," MacIntyre said to Mrs. Chant. "That's not too much to ask of anyone is it?" (Barss Donham 1989: 182). Mrs. Chant agreed that it was not and instructed her son to tell the truth. Chant realized he had lied to the police the last time he was questioned and now wanted to be honest. He told MacIntyre that the only thing he knew about the stabbing was what Marshall told him on Byng Avenue shortly after Seale was wounded. MacIntyre was angered at this revelation and told Chant that the police had an eyewitness that saw him in the park at the time. This was a lie of course. Chant had not been in the park and no one had claimed to have seen him there.

MacIntyre again broke police regulations by asking Mrs. Chant to leave the room so the police could question Chant alone. MacIntyre then resorted to intimidation techniques, threatening to jail the fourteen-year-old (who was on probation for petty theft) if he did not tell everything he knew. Chant, crying and scared, maintained he saw nothing. As was the case with Pratico, Maynard Chant slowly succumbed to the pressure and began to piece together what it was the police wanted to hear. Near the end of the session MacIntyre began to record Maynard Chant's heinous lie. Chant's claim now was that he had been walking down the railroad tracks when he saw a dark-haired youth, John Pratico, crouched behind some bushes watching something on Crescent Street. He looked across to Crescent Street and saw two men standing close together. One of these he recognized as Donald Marshall Jr. The two men were arguing and Marshall drew a knife from his pocket and drove it into the right side of Seale's stomach. Marshall then ran from the scene toward Byng Avenue. It was at this point that Marshall caught up to Chant and showed him the wound on his arm.

It was the perfect story for MacIntyre. Not only did it have Marshall stabbing Seale, but it confirmed Pratico as the second eyewitness to the crime. This was all the evidence MacIntyre needed and he quickly presented it to Crown Prosecutor Donald MacNeil. An arrest warrant was issued for Donald Marshall and he was picked up at home, handcuffed and driven back to Sydney. "I didn't do it" was all he said to the officers (Barss Donham 1989: 185).

The police were ignoring eyewitness reports that did not jive with the statements of Chant and Portico. Two teenagers, George and Roderick MacNeil (no relation to Jimmy or Donald), had reported to police that they had seen two men fitting Marshall's description of Roy Ebsary and Jimmy MacNeil in the park around midnight. The statements of Terry Gushue and Patricia Harriss, also mentioned the two men who were with Marshall and Seale shortly before the killing. Gushue admitted to being quite drunk at the time so it was easy to dismiss his account of the evening, but Harriss had been sober and had vivid memories of Ebsary and MacNeil, which presented a problem for the police.

Harriss's descriptions of the two men she had seen with Marshall and MacNeil were identical to Marshall's descriptions. If the police were to have a clean case against Marshall it was essential that Patricia Harriss abandon her original statement. After nearly five hours of intimidating interrogation by MacIntyre and Urquhart, Harriss caved in. All she wanted was to get out of this terrible situation and the only way she could see to do that was to tell the police what they wanted to hear. Her new statement made no mention of seeing anyone resembling Ebsary and MacNeil, while she claimed to have seen Marshall and Seale alone on Crescent Street just before the time of the murder. There were no longer any complicating factors in the police case against Marshall: Maynard Chant, John Pratico and Patricia Harriss were all going to give the same eyewitness account of the crime in court. A preliminary hearing into the case was held in June and Marshall was bound over for trial on November 2, 1971. Shortly after Marshall's arrest the atmosphere in the community was heavy with racial overtones. The Marshall family was inundated with so many threatening phone calls that Donald Marshall Sr. temporarily moved his family out of the community.

THE TRIAL

If the police seemed convinced they had a tight case against Donald Marshall, Crown Prosecutor Donald MacNeil may not have been as confident. The best evidence available to the Crown was the eyewitness testimony of three teenagers who had been pressured by the police to tell the same story. Furthermore, one of the three, John Pratico was schizophrenic and had been admitted to a mental hospital in Dartmouth shortly after the preliminary hearing. He returned to Sydney a week before the trial under heavy medication. In an attempt to ensure conformity, the prosecutor had both Pratico and Chant review their stories prior to the trial. The third witness, Patricia Harriss, did not receive the same attention. As a result, her testimony proved to be considerably less supportive of the Crown's case.

The prosecutor was counting on Harriss to testify that she had observed Marshall and Seale alone together in the park the evening of the murder. But Harriss wanted to tell the court what she knew to be the truth. When she took the stand to testify the prosecutor asked her if she had seen more than one person with Marshall. The answer he expected was a simple "no." He was shocked when she responded "yes" (Harris 1986: 151; Barss Donham 1989: 189). Knowing Harriss's testimony could cause him to lose the case, the prosecutor's tone became more intimidating. Harriss's resolve to tell the truth was no match for MacNeil's courtroom skills and she quickly reverted back to her fabricated testimony, saying that she had seen no one except Marshall and Seale in the park.

Marshall's defence lawyer, C.M. Rosenblum had been given the

35

case by the federal Department of Indian Affairs. For reasons unknown, he had not interviewed any of the prosecution's star witnesses before the trial and was therefore unaware of the statements they had initially given to the police. Since he knew nothing of Harriss's original statement concerning the gray-haired man she had seen with Marshall and Seale, he did not pursue this line of questioning when he cross-examined her. Instead, he emphasized the flimsy quality of her testimony and had her agree that she was not sure if the person seen with Marshall had been a man, woman or child.

If Patricia Harriss's performance on the stand was less than the prosecution had expected, Maynard Chant was to add to their problems. At the preliminary inquiry Chant had claimed that he recognized Marshall and Seale as the two people in the park and that they were having a bitter argument. He also stated that he had seen Marshall take a knife from his pocket and stab Seale. At the trial Chant told the prosecutor that he thought he heard two people arguing in the park but he did not know who they were. He added that one of the men had taken something from his pocket and drove it towards the left side of the other man.

Chant's testimony was almost useless for the prosecution's case against Marshall. In desperation, Crown Prosecutor MacNeil asked the judge to declare Chant a hostile witness. Such a ruling would give the prosecution the right to cross-examine its own witness. Although the defence objected that there was little legal justification for this move, Judge Louis Dubinsky agreed to the request.

MacNeil suggested to Chant that the testimony he had given at the preliminary hearing was considerably different from his present recollection of events. He then refreshed Chant's memory by reading his original testimony to the court. Chant knew that he faced a charge of perjury if he denied the original testimony. MacNeil's intimidating style was once more sufficient to cause Chant to revert back to his preliminary hearing testimony, stating that he had seen Marshall stab Seale with a knife.

Meanwhile, John Pratico was waiting outside the courtroom to testify. His conscience was bothering him. He knew that his statement to the police had been a lie and that if he repeated it in court he would be helping to convict Marshall of a crime he did not commit. He wanted to tell the truth. In a spontaneous act of bravery

Pratico approached Donald Marshall Sr., who was also in the corridor, and told him that he knew Marshall did not kill Seale. Stunned by this revelation, Marshall Sr. had Pratico repeat the statement to Simon Khattar, a member of the defence team, who then had him repeat it to the sheriff who was standing nearby. The little group in the corridor quickly grew to include Crown Prosecutor MacNeil and Sergeant MacIntyre.

Ushered into a small antechamber, Pratico once more repeated his observation that Marshall did not stab Seale and that he had lied to the police and to the prosecution because he was scared. Both MacIntyre and MacNeil demanded to know if he was suggesting that they had threatened him. Pratico said they had not, but it was obvious to Khattar that Pratico was indeed terrified by the two men. He tried to reassure the teenager and told him not to be afraid of anyone but to just tell the truth to the court.

Pratico took the stand and MacNeil began to question him about the statement made in the corridor. However, Judge Dubinsky insisted that MacNeil confine his questioning to the events in Wentworth Park. The judge's instruction worked to the prosecution's advantage. MacNeil asked Pratico to tell the court exactly what he had witnessed the night of May 28. Khattar's heart sank as the youth related that he had seen Marshall kill Seale. It would seem that the teenager's desire to tell the truth had been overcome by his fear of MacNeil and MacIntyre.

Cross-examined by Khattar the next day Pratico admitted to the recantation in the corridor. However, Judge Dubinsky, citing and incorrectly interpreting a section of the Canadian Evidence Act, ruled that Khattar could not fully question Pratico on his corridor statement. But Dubinsky did allow the prosecution to ask Pratico why he had made the comments in the corridor. Pratico's simple response to the question was that he was afraid for his life. Judge Dubinsky's faulty interpretation of the Canada Evidence Act and his ruling that Khattar could not question Pratico about the corridor conversation had allowed the prosecution to imply that Pratico had made the comments because Marshall Sr. had threatened him. Nothing could have been further from the truth but, shielded from the facts of the encounter, the jury was predisposed to believe the prosecution. Rosenblum and Khattar now realized they had little choice but to put Marshall on the stand.

Rosenblum asked Marshall to tell the jury about the events of May 28. Marshall related the story of how they had met two men on Crescent Street and stopped to ask them for a light. One of the men was old and dressed like a priest, the other was younger. The men said they were from Manitoba and then said they did not like Indians or Blacks. They then assaulted Marshall and Seale. But Marshall's testimony was so disjointed and erratic that he did his case irreparable harm. As he left the stand many of those on the jury may have had good reason to believe that the young Mi'kmaw was Sandy Seale's killer.

After the defence and the prosecution gave their summations, the jury retired to consider its verdict. Four hours later the jury found Donald Marshall guilty of second degree murder. He was sentenced to life in prison.

THE STRUGGLE FOR FREEDOM AND TRUTH

Donald Marshall Jr. was an innocent man sentenced to life imprisonment on the basis of police interrogation procedures and perjured evidence. John Pratico and Maynard Chant swore that they had seen Marshall stab Sandy Seale. Patricia Harriss likewise swore that she had seen Marshall and Seale alone in the park. All three witnesses were to later recant their testimony, claiming they had been intimidated by the police to the point that they would say whatever the police wanted them to say on the witness stand.

Had it not been for the perseverance of RCMP Staff Sergeant Harry Wheaton and a few other members of the force, Donald Marshall Jr. may very well still be in prison. In the process of discovering the truth in the Marshall case, Wheaton and the others exposed the dark side of the Canadian justice system. During the many years that Donald Marshall was serving time in prison, many people attempted to correct the wrong that had been done to the young Mi'kmaw. One of these was Jimmy MacNeil, the young man who had been with Ebsary the night the old man stabbed Sandy Seale.

MacNeil and Ebsary had run the 400 yards from the crime scene to Ebsary's home immediately after Seale had fallen to the ground. Excited and terrified by the events he had just witnessed, MacNeil did not know whether Ebsary was a hero who had just saved his life or a madman who had committed cold-blooded murder. As they slammed the door of the house behind them Ebsary's wife Mary instinctively knew her husband was in one of his bad moods. Not wanting a family fight she sent Donna, their fourteen-year-old daughter, to bed. But MacNeil was babbling on about the night's adventure and Donna decided to spy on them. She was gripped with both fear and fascination as she watched her father standing at the kitchen sink washing blood from one of his homemade knives. Donna would carry this secret with her for many years before relating it to the authorities.

Jimmy MacNeil suffered the agony of his guilty conscience almost immediately after Marshall's conviction. When his brother John arrived home for a visit in early November 1971, Jimmy was in the depths of a severe depression. After a little probing from his brother, the dam broke and Jimmy spilled out his story. His brother insisted he go to the police. A few hours later Jimmy was relating the true events of the murder to John MacIntyre. McNeil's description of Ebsary was almost identical to the man described by Donald Marshall. Patricia Harriss had also initially described such a man before she was pressured by the police to change her story. Obviously MacIntyre had to act on this information so he contacted Assistant Prosecutor Lew Matheson.

Matheson read McNeil's statement and ordered the detectives to pick up Ebsary and his family. While interviewing Ebsary's wife, the detective did not pursue some of the information about Ebsary's activities as related to him by McNeil. He failed to ask if her husband ever carried a knife or if she had seen him washing blood from a knife the evening of May 28. MacIntyre also failed to interview the one person who *had* seen Ebsary washing the bloody knife—Ebsary's daughter, Donna.

MacIntyre interviewed Roy Ebsary on the same evening. Yes, he remembered the evening well. He and Jimmy MacNeil had been accosted in the park that evening by two men who wanted their money. After a short altercation he and McNeil had managed to beat the two men off and they ran away. Ebsary further stated that he certainly did not stab anyone that night and at no time did he carry a knife on his person. MacIntyre's acceptance of this statement is interesting because Ebsary had been arrested by the police department several months earlier for carrying a concealed knife. It is not known whether MacIntyre knew this and ignored the fact or whether he had not bothered to check Ebsary's record before he questioned him.

Meanwhile, Robert Anderson, the Nova Scotia director of criminal investigations, had been informed of Jimmy MacNeil's confession and decided to solicit the assistance of the RCMP. The Mounties sent Sub-Inspector Alan Marshall to assist in sorting out the investigation. The inspector listened to John MacIntyre's views on the murder and interviewed Jimmy MacNeil. He did not bother to interview Ebsary, the man singled out by Jimmy MacNeil as Seale's killer. But he did subject both Ebsary and MacNeil to a polygraph test. MacNeil was so nervous during the test that the results were useless. Ebsary on the other hand passed the test with ease, giving absolutely no indication he was lying when he denied killing Sandy Seale. In writing his final report 1972, Alan Marshall was obviously swayed by the polygraph results. Jimmy MacNeil, he concluded, was a young man of low intelligence who only imagined that he had seen Ebsary stab Seale. The unwritten inference of the report was that the justice system had not erred when it convicted Donald Marshall Jr.

During the RCMP investigation, Marshall's lawyer Moe Rosenblum had been preparing an appeal for his client; an appeal he did not think he could win. Had Rosenblum known of Jimmy MacNeil's statement and the fact that John Pratico, one of the prosecution's star witnesses, had been admitted to a Dartmouth mental hospital while suffering from severe paranoid delusions, he may have had a more positive outlook. Ignorant of these important facts, the lawyer was unable to pass them on to the Appeal Division of the Supreme Court. The court turned down the appeal in early September 1972. If the formal participants in the Marshall case thought the final chapter had been written, they were wrong.

Over the next decade certain events began to unfold that were to make the trial and conviction of Donald Marshall Jr. one of the most celebrated cases in the annals of Canadian legal history. Donna Ebsary, Roy Ebsary's daughter, played a major role in these events. Fourteen-year-old Donna had seen her father washing blood from a knife in their kitchen sink the night Seale was murdered. Three years later, as a more mature seventeen-year-old, she desperately wanted to tell what she had seen to someone she could trust. She found that person in David Ratchford, who operated the martial arts school she was attending. Because Donna was afraid, Ratchford agreed to go to the police on her behalf. When he told the story to John MacIntyre and William Urquhart, he was told the case was closed and they had no interest in talking to Donna.

At about the same time, it was becoming obvious to Mary Ebsary that her husband was displaying a growing sexual preference for young men. When he brought young Mitchell Sarson home to live with him and became increasingly rowdy and obnoxious, Mary tossed them both out of the house. Before the relationship between the two men ended, Ebsary had told Sarson about the time he had stabbed a man in the park.

Coincidentally, Donald Marshall had developed a relationship with Mitchell Sarson's sister, Shelly. In 1981 Mitchell accompanied her on one of her prison visits to Marshall. As Mitchell listened to Marshall and Shelly talking he realized just how important his previous relationship with Ebsary might be to Marshall. Mitchell told Marshall that Roy Ebsary had once confided to him that he had killed an Afro-Canadian man in Wentworth Park and wounded an Indian during the same incident. It was an unbelievable moment for Marshall; after years of telling people that an unknown old man with a beard was the actual killer of Sandy Seale, Donald Marshall now had that man's name. The long process of proving his own innocence had finally begun.

It would be six months before the authorities began to act on this new evidence. Had it not been for the intervention of the Union of Nova Scotia Indians, the delays may have gone on indefinitely. The union had retained lawyer Stephen Aronson to follow up on Marshall's story. Aronson met with Mitchell Sarson and heard his story about Roy Ebsary's confession. He also discovered that the Sydney police had arrested Roy Ebsary in 1981 for stabbing another man. When Aronson asked MacIntyre (who had become Sydney's police chief in 1976) to check out Sarson's story, the chief became defensive. He told Crown Prosecutor Frank Edwards and Inspector Don Scott, the man in charge of Sydney's RCMP detachment, that Marshall's conviction was soundly based on the eyewitness reports of two individuals. He stated that Sarson's story was obviously a fabrication because Marshall was romantically involved with his sister. The chief gave the RCMP some files relating to the case and told him to check things out for himself.

Scott asked Staff Sergeant Harry Wheaton to assist him on the case. After talking to MacIntyre, Wheaton initially thought that Marshall was guilty. However, when he learned that Ebsary had been convicted of carrying a concealed weapon in 1971 and charged with stabbing a man in 1982, he began to have some nagging doubts. Mary Ebsary confirmed that Roy Ebsary and Mitchell Sarson had a brief relationship in 1971. Wheaton now felt he could be on to something worth pursuing.

Mitchell Sarson told Wheaton and Corporal Jim Carroll that he and Ebsary had a brief relationship and that Ebsary had told him he had killed an Afro-Canadian man in the park. The two policemen now had strong reason to believe that Donald Marshall's claims of innocence were true. But if MacNeil and Sarson were telling the truth, that meant that the eyewitness testimonies of John Pratico and Maynard Chant had been perjured.

Wheaton and Carroll found Maynard Chant working at a Louisbourg fish plant. Chant told the officers that he had been pressured by the police into saying that he had seen Marshall kill Seale. He indicated that MacIntyre in particular had intimidated him. Wheaton and Carroll were stunned by the fact that a key witness for the prosecution was now saying that he had been under pressure from the Sydney police and presented perjured testimony on the stand.

John Pratico was no longer living at home but his mother suggested that Wheaton speak to her son's social worker or psychiatrist. Wheaton contacted Pratico's psychiatrist and was told that Pratico was a schizophrenic who would have been a very unreliable witness at Marshall's trial. Wheaton also discovered that Pratico had been placed in a mental institution shortly after the trial. It was only some time later that Carroll located Pratico through a psychiatric social worker who had Pratico as a client. Carroll arranged an interview with Pratico, who admitted he had perjured himself on the stand. He said he had done so because the police had told him he would be put in jail if he did not sign a statement saying he had seen Marshall stab Sandy Seale.

On February 18, 1982, Wheaton and Carroll interviewed Marshall in Dorchester Penitentiary. What he told them confirmed their belief that he was innocent. Furthermore, it now seemed clear that Roy Ebsary was the real killer. Both Wheaton and Carroll wanted to talk to the man who had evaded justice for so long and had knowingly let Donald Marshall serve time for a crime he himself had committed. However, the subsequent interview with Ebsary was little more than a drunken rambling. All Ebsary would say to Carroll was that if

Marshall were to have a new trial he would be willing to give evidence. This statement was better than nothing but, given Ebsary's propensity to lie, there could be no assurance that the man would tell the truth in court.

When RCMP Inspector Scott confronted MacIntyre with the new evidence, especially the recantations of Pratico and Chant, MacIntyre claimed they must be lying and pointed to Patricia Harriss's 1971 statement that she had seen Marshall and Seale alone in Wentworth Park just before the murder. The Mounties had not been previously told of Harriss' statement and Scott began to suspect that MacIntyre may have withheld other material. Scott requested that all relevant information be turned over to him. He also wanted to interview Patricia Harriss and get her version of the events in Wentworth Park.

When Wheaton interviewed Harriss on March 1, 1982, she indicated that she had been bothered about her role in the case for eleven years. She said that the Sydney police took several statements from her in 1971 and changed them to suit their version of the murder. She confessed that she felt scared and intimidated by the police and had said things in court that were not true. In truth, she had seen Donald Marshall on Crescent Street with several other men on the night of the murder. She had not seen Marshall alone with Seale as she had told the court. Wheaton now had all three key witnesses for the prosecution admitting that they had given perjured testimony at the trial because they had been coerced by MacIntyre.

Greg Ebsary, Roy's son, had shown Wheaton a number of knives that his father had made before the murder. Wheaton sent them off to the RCMP laboratories in Halifax with the hope that traces of Seale's blood could be found on one of them. The lab report confirmed that one of the knives contained several fibres from Sandy Seale's jacket. There were also a lesser number of fibres matching those of the jacket worn by Donald Marshall.

On April 5, 1982, the Crown prosecutor recommended that Ebsary be charged with murder and that the process of freeing Marshall be implemented. But the wheels of justice grind slowly. Some very nervous individuals within the judicial bureaucracy attempted to impede Marshall's appeal, while others attempted to stonewall any inquiry into police misconduct. Had people like Wheaton and Carroll not been so determined to see justice properly served, it is possible that Donald Marshall's name would never have been cleared and the reprehensible behaviour of the Sydney police would have remained undetected.

The appeal hearing began December 1, 1982. Marshall's lawyer, Stephen Aronson, attempted to have Marshall tell the court everything that happened the evening of the murder, including the fact that he and Seale had gone to the park with the intent of getting some money from people. Prosecutor Edwards pushed the point, suggesting that Marshall and Seale had intended to mug someone that evening. Marshall admitted that they had agreed to get money regardless of the method, but denied carrying through with the intention. As the hearing progressed Edwards seemed less intent on proving Marshall innocent of murder than he was proving him guilty of robbery. This was an exceptional turn of events because Marshall had never been charged with robbery. When Aronson objected to the line of questioning, he was overruled. Maynard Chant and Patricia Harriss took the stand and recanted their 1971 testimonies. The RCMP forensic expert, Adolphus Evers, testified that the cloth fibres found on Ebsary's knife matched the jackets of Sandy Seale and Donald Marshall, and Donna Ebsary told the court that she had seen her father washing blood from a knife the evening of the murder.

Despite all the evidence to the contrary, Crown Prosecutor Edwards sensed that the five appeal court judges were hesitant to rule it a miscarriage of justice and would not recommend an outright acquittal. At best, he thought they would order a new trial: a trial the prosecution could not win because there was simply no longer any evidence that would link Donald Marshall to the crime. Edwards had to come up with an approach that would avoid a new trial but ensure that Marshall was acquitted. To placate the judges, Edwards would adopted the premise that Marshall had not been the victim of a miscarriage of justice. He argued that Marshall ensured his own conviction because he had not informed the court or his lawyers that he and Sandy Seale had planned a robbery in the park. To further appease the five judges, he insisted that the Sydney police force had acted with propriety in the case, displaying no malicious intent toward Marshall. In his summation he argued that, since there was no evidence that Marshall had committed the murder, the court should acquit him.

Some may question whether Edwards' interpretation of the facts represent a responsible action on the part of a Crown prosecutor.

Most certainly Donald Marshall must have been angered by the suggestion that he brought about his own incarceration and that the Sydney police had acted without malice. What Marshall did not know was that Edwards had put his own job in jeopardy by arguing for the acquittal. Deputy Attorney General Gordon Coles was a powerful political figure in the province and Edwards' superior. When he heard of Edwards' intention to seek an acquittal, he summoned him to his office and demanded that instead of asking for an acquittal Edwards simply take no position. Coles threatened to take him off the case if Edwards insisted on proceeding with the acquittal.

Edwards broke with tradition and used some threats of his own. He told Coles that if he was forced to take no position in the appeal, he would inform the court that he was doing so under orders from the deputy attorney general. Such a public revelation would have been a political disaster for Coles. He had little choice but to acquiesce to Edwards' position. The appeal court reconvened in February and heard both Aronson and Edwards argue for Donald Marshall's acquittal on the grounds that there was no evidence of his guilt. Three months later the appeal court came down with its decision that no reasonable jury could find Marshall guilty based on the evidence and, twelve years after his arrest, Donald Marshall Jr. was acquitted.

But the five appeal judges were not about to admit a miscarriage of justice had taken place. In their summation the judges noted that in relation to the Marshall case "any miscarriage of justice is more apparent than real" (Harris 1986: 368). Marshall's arrest and conviction were rationalized as being a product of his own lies and evasions during the course of the investigation and trial. The court concluded, ". . . Donald Marshall's untruthfulness through this whole affair contributed in large measure to his conviction" (Nova Scotia Supreme Court 1983).

As for the real killer, Roy Ebsary was to stand trial three times for the second degree murder of Sandy Seale. His first trial resulted in a hung jury; the second, in a conviction, which was overturned by appeal; the third, again in a conviction. On appeal his three-year sentence was reduced to one year. He served seven months and died in his Sydney rooming house of a heart attack at the age of seventy-five. It is an interesting comment on the justice system that a young Mi'kmaw was sentenced to life in prison for a crime for which an older non-Indian later received a one year sentence.

WHY WAS DONALD MARSHALL WRONGFULLY CONVICTED?

Donald Marshall became central to the police investigation of the case from the moment Seale was stabbed. He was an eyewitness to the event and had himself sustained an injury when he was slashed by the killer. The fact that homicide was a rare event in Sydney meant that the police had little experience in this area of crime and made some serious errors. For example, when the police first arrived on the scene Seale was still alive and conscious. If a police officer had accompanied Seale in the ambulance on the way to the hospital, Seale could have told the officer who stabbed him. However, no officer rode in the ambulance and the doctors at the hospital would not allow the police to question Seale, who died without making a statement. The scene of the crime was not searched that evening nor were the names of people in the park recorded by the police. Furthermore, the description of Ebsary given to the police by Marshall on the evening of the murder was not recorded and circulated to other members of the Sydney police.

Even more important was the antagonism between Donald Marshall Jr. and Sergeant of Detectives John MacIntyre. MacIntyre knew Marshall from his previous run-ins with the law and the two did not like each other. Before interviewing witnesses MacIntyre concluded that Marshall was the person responsible for the murder. From this point on, the police would ignore eyewitness reports and other evidence that did not fit this version of the story.

Another disturbing aspect of this case is the tactics used by the police to obtain false testimony from vulnerable young people. John Pratico's only knowledge of the stabbing was limited to what Marshall had told him and what he had heard on the radio. But the police pressured the young man into signing a fabricated account of the events in Wentworth Park by threatening him with jail. Maynard Chant informed the police that he knew only what Marshall had told him about the stabbing. The police insisted that Chant's mother leave the room so they could interrogate Chant without her being present (a breach of police regulations). They then threatened the fourteen-year-old with jail until the terrified young man fabricated the facts they wanted to hear. Patricia Harriss had been telling the truth when she informed the police that she had seen Ebsary and MacNeil with Marshall and Seale in the park the night of the murder. Because her statement did not support the police theory that Marshall and Seale were in the park alone, the police continued to interrogate her until she told them what they wanted to hear. The key element in the Crown's case against Marshall was to be the coerced and false testimony of these three young people. When the RCMP reopened the case, the Sydney police initially withheld important files and other information.

In addition to police malfeasance, the numerous judicial errors by Trial Judge Dubinsky, particularly his misinterpretation of the Canada Evidence Act, were detrimental to the legal interest of Donald Marshall Jr. We must also consider the conduct of Crown Prosecutor Donald MacNeil, who had not disclosed the totality of the Crown's case to the defence as the law requires. Even officials in the Halifax attorney general's office were accused by the Royal Commission of failing to discharge their duties.

The wrongful conviction of Donald Marshall Jr. resulted from police targeting and legal incompetence on the part of the attorney general's office, the prosecution, the defence and the judiciary. These factors alone may have been sufficient to convict Donald Marshall Jr. of Sandy Seale's murder, but when combined with the systemic racism and bigotry characteristic of Sydney in 1971, Marshall had little chance of being found innocent.

The arrest and conviction of Donald Marshall is a perfect illustration of the systemic classism, racism and social injustice that permeates not only our system of justice, but Canadian society as a whole. The Marshall case highlights two things. First, that the justice system is prepared to proceed on the presumption of guilt rather than innocence if the accused is a member of a marginalized minority group, and second, as Ratner, McMullan and Burtch (1987) so aptly point out, when the authority of the state is challenged by public opinion as it was in the Marshall case, it seeks first to protect its own interests.

Joy Mannette makes the comment that "[w]hile from Marshall's perspective the system failed miserably, for most of the citizens of Sydney it worked to perfection: a clean solution to a very dirty incident with all the safeguards of the system observed and speedy justice prevailing" (Mannette 1992: 25). Mannette further notes that, even when it became obvious that the Sydney police had got the wrong man, the public believed Marshall's conviction was simply the result of malevolent action on the part of some individual police officers. Public faith in the system had been only slightly tarnished and it was felt that this could be corrected by admitting a mistake had occurred and awarding some compensation to Marshall (Mannette 1994). However, when the appeal court blamed Marshall for his own conviction, the public was outraged. It appeared that the court was more concerned about protecting the justice system's image and its officials than assisting Donald Marshall Jr. in gaining an apology and compensation. Only when the public outcry against this judicial whitewash became too loud to ignore did the government appoint a Royal Commission to investigate the Marshall affair.

The Royal Commission on the Donald Marshall Junior Prosecution began hearings on September 9, 1987. Because public faith in the Nova Scotia's judicial system was at a very low ebb after the Marshall fiasco, it was essential that any possibility of a conflict of interest among the various levels of the Nova Scotia system be avoided. This could be assured in part by appointing senior justice officials from other provinces to head the commission. While it was obvious that the commission's investigation was important to Donald Marshall Jr., it was equally obvious that the justice system itself was on trial. The $8-million, seven-volume report, released January 26, 1990, was a damning indictment of Nova Scotia's criminal justice system and the inequality and racism that had infested the entire social structure of the region.

Casting aside the muted language usually required of such official reports, the commissioners observed that the arrest, trial and conviction of Donald Marshall resulted from the incompetence of the police, lawyers and officials higher up in Nova Scotia's judicial system. It was noted that the police investigation of the Marshall case was "entirely inadequate, incompetent and unprofessional" and that the eyewitness testimonies of Maynard Chant, John Pratico and Patricia Harriss were the product of police intimidation. Their report also blasted Trial Judge Dubinsky for his incompetence during the trial, Crown Prosecutor Donald MacNeil for failing to fully disclose the Crown's case to the defence team, and defence lawyer Moe Rosenblum for his failure to adequately represent his client. The report concluded that one of the reasons the report failed Marshall was because he was native (Royal Commission on the Donald Marshall Junior Prosecution, 1989: 1). The reasons for Donald Marshall Jr.'s wrongful conviction cannot be limited to some professional or bureaucratic wrong-doing. The police, lawyers, judges and politicians involved in the case carried out their actions in a society plagued with racism and bigotry; a society that did not care about truth and justice. A society that did not care about Donald Marshall Jr.

James "Sakej" Youngblood Henderson indicates clearly how the testimony of witnesses at the Royal Commission Inquiry confirms the racism existing in Nova Scotia in 1971:

> Staff Wheaton of the R.C.M.P. testified that he had originally disagreed with the characterization of Sydney, Nova Scotia, as having a "redneck atmosphere." But after his investigation with a cross section of people (for example, educators, lawyers, doctors, merchants, and others) about racism in Sydney in 1971 . . . he found that such an atmosphere existed and may have played on the jury's mind (Henderson 1992: 42).

Even the local judges and Crown prosecutors maintained racist attitudes towards the local Mi'kmaq population. '

> Continually, the local prosecutors and judges complained that the "Indian" youth "did not know their place" in society. The "Indians" did not belong in Sydney and merely came to upset the peace and quiet. It was alleged by a court worker that a local judge stated in court that a fence should be built around the Eskassoni Reserve so that "Indians could not get out to come to Sydney to cause problems" (Henderson 1992: 42)

The author also notes that "[w]hen Staff Sergeant Wheaton asked Chief of Police MacIntyre why he thought Chant lied in the first instance, in addition to his personal fear of Junior Marshall, MacIntyre indicated Chant was afraid of Indians" (Henderson 1992: 42).

In concluding their report, the commissioners tell us very specifically why Donald Marshall became a victim of the system:

> The criminal justice system failed Donald Marshall at virtually every turn, from his arrest and wrongful conviction for

murder in 1971 up to and even beyond his acquittal by the Court of Appeal in 1983. The tragedy of the failure is compounded by the evidence that this miscarriage of justice could and should have been prevented, or at least corrected quickly, if those involved in the system had carried out their duties in a professional and/or competent manner. That they did not is due, in part at least, to the fact that Donald Marshall Jr. is a Native" (Royal Commission, 1989: 1).

Even this damning indictment by the Royal Commission has not deterred attempts to deflect the social inequality issue and restore the credibility of the justice system. Shortly after the Royal Commission submitted its report, Deputy Attorney General Gordon Coles tried to dampen its political impact by suggesting that Marshall's release from prison after eleven years of wrongful incarceration was proof that the system worked. Donald Marshall may well disagree.

NOTE

1. Those wishing more details regarding the Donald Marshall case are encouraged to read Harris 1986 and Barss Donham 1989. Most of the information in this chapter was derived from these sources.

3

The Case
of David Milgaard

THE DEFENDANT

David Milgaard was a child of the sixties. At sixteen years of age he appeared to be the perfect stereotype of the self-centered, long-haired hippie revelling in a life of free love and soft drugs. Like many of his friends, he flouted the law, selling drugs, stealing cars and breaking into homes and businesses to meet his needs (*Regina Leader Post*: April 13, 1992). He dropped out of school and became a drifter. His free and easy approach to sex earned him the name "Hoppy" among his friends, because he was forever hopping in and out of bed (*Regina Leader Post*: April 13, 1992).

But there was more to Milgaard than the thin veneer of his "hippie" persona suggested. Even before his teenage years he had been in constant trouble. His parents withdrew him from kindergarten because he was a negative influence on the other children. The schools he attended labeled him as an impulsive, restless troublemaker who often fought with other students and resisted authority (*Regina Leader Post*: April 13, 1992). By the time he was thirteen he had spent three months in a regional psychiatric centre. When released he was so difficult to handle that his parents did not want him at home and he was placed in a series of foster homes and a boys' school. Life in the small town of Langenburg, Saskatchewan, was boring and unappealing. He was attracted to the bohemian youth culture that provided a home to countless alienated and marginalized teens. At sixteen years of age he was travelling the country with his friends in search of new and exciting experiences. It was this search that placed him in Saskatoon on the morning of January 31, 1969.

THE CRIME

That January morning, the temperature had plunged to minus forty degrees in Saskatoon. Eleven-year-old Alice Marcoux had dressed for the cold before leaving her home and heading to school at 8:30 a.m. Taking a shortcut through an alley, she noticed something in the snow. It was the body of twenty-year-old Gail Miller, a nursing assistant at Saskatoon's City Hospital. Police quickly determined that the young woman was the victim of a brutal rape and murder.

Miller had left her rooming house in a working-class district of Saskatoon at about 6:45 a.m. and was walking to a nearby bus stop when she was attacked and dragged into the alley. When police searched the area they found what they believed to be the murder weapon, a blood-stained blade that appeared to have come from a kitchen paring knife. The coroner's report disclosed that Miller had been stabbed in the back, front, sides and neck a total of twelve times and had also suffered numerous nonfatal slash wounds. Forensic evidence also suggested that the rape had occurred after her death. Time of death was estimated to be between 6:45 a.m and 7:30 a.m.[1]

Few clues to the murder emerged. Miller's purse was found in a nearby garbage can; there was no money in it. No incriminating fingerprints were found and there was no evidence that Miller knew anyone who would do her any harm. It appeared that Miller had been the victim of a person or persons unknown and that this person was still at large, possibly still in the city.

Murders in Saskatoon were not a common event in the sixties. The media gave the Miller murder considerable attention. Rumours began to spread in the community that other attacks and rapes had taken place and that a mad killer was in their midst. Indeed, two sexual attacks on women had occurred in the same area of the city as the Miller murder. The similarities of these attacks to the Miller case had not escaped police attention but, not wanting to swell public hysteria, the authorities attempted to suppress this information. Nonetheless, public fear and panic continued to grow and the Saskatoon police felt the pressure to solve the case. Having no obvious suspects, the police offered a $2,000 reward to anyone with information that would lead to the conviction of Gail Miller's killer. It was this reward that was to draw David Milgaard's name into the case.

During the last week of January 1969, David Milgaard had drifted into Regina where he ran into Ron Wilson, an old friend. Since

52

Wilson had been given a 1958 Pontiac for Christmas, he and Milgaard decided that an extended trip to Alberta was in order. They had little difficulty persuading sixteen-year-old Nichol John to quit her waitressing job and accompany them. After repairing the tires and stealing a battery the trio left Regina shortly past midnight on January 31 bound for Saskatoon, where Milgaard wanted to pick up his friend Albert "Shorty" Cadrain. They arrived in Saskatoon between 5:30 and 6:30 in the morning. An interpretation of events immediately following their arrival in Saskatoon would determine David Milgaard's life for the next twenty-three years.

John and Wilson had never been to Saskatoon before, while Milgaard had only a vague idea of where Cadrain lived. They drove around aimlessly, asking questions of one woman who was unable to help them, and then picked up a city map from a local motel. Guided by the map, they returned to Cadrain's neighbourhood. There they encountered Walter Danchuk, a local resident whose car was stuck in the snow. They tried to push his car free. Instead both cars became stuck and, in the effort to free them, Milgaard ripped his pants. Danchuk took the three into his house and called for a tow truck. It was 7:30 in the morning. An hour later both cars were freed and the three continued on to Cadrain's home. It was located at 334 Avenue O, a short distance from where Gail Miller's body had been found. Living in the basement suite were Larry Fisher and his wife Linda. Fisher would later be found guilty of several vicious rapes in Saskatoon and Winnipeg.

Cadrain agreed to accompany Milgaard and his friends on their trip. Before they left, Milgaard changed his ripped pants in full view of his friends. The group then left the house and drove the car to a garage to have the transmission repaired. By 4:30 that afternoon they were on their way to Alberta. The group was in Alberta only a few days, returning to Regina on February 5. A few days later Cadrain was arrested by the Regina police for vagrancy and sentenced to a week in jail. Meanwhile, the Saskatoon police had received a tip that a group of young people had been at the Cadrain house in Saskatoon on the day of the murder. When the Regina police questioned him about the murder, they learned nothing. He was back on the streets in a few days but this was not the last the police were to see of him.

By early March, Cadrain had returned to Saskatoon where he heard of the $2,000 reward in the Miller case. He immediately went to the

Saskatoon police with a most intriguing version of the events of January 31. Cadrain told the police that Milgaard had blood on his clothes when he arrived at the Cadrain residence and seemed to be in a hurry to leave town (Hughes 1992). He also told the police that, on the way to Alberta, Milgaard had thrown a woman's cosmetic case from the car and told him that he would have to get rid of Wilson and John because they knew too much. Cadrain would later collect the reward money.

Sensing they were on to something big, the police tracked down Ron Wilson and Nichol John. Wilson indicated Milgaard did not have blood on his clothes that morning and had not been away from the group long enough to commit the murder. Interviewed separately, John supported Wilson's version of the event. Nevertheless, the police pursued Milgaard, tracking him down in Prince George, British Columbia, where he had secured a job selling magazine subscriptions. He was questioned several times, giving the same story as Wilson and John.

However, the police were not finished questioning them. Wilson, who was only seventeen at the time, was interrogated repeatedly by both the Saskatoon and Regina police. Over three weeks he was given a polygraph test; shown Gail Miller's blood-stained clothes; taken to the scene of the crime; and subjected to a particularly stressful interview, during which he and John were interrogated together. During the interrogation procedures, Wilson began to suspect that he was being fed information by the police, which they wanted repeated back to them in a sworn statement. This information conformed to the police's version of the events of January 31 and would implicate Milgaard as Miller's killer. The police continued the intense pressure and relentless interrogations to the point that Wilson's resolve to tell the truth crumbled. Bit by bit he began to implicate Milgaard, fabricating a story from the morsels of information fed to him by the police.

Not only did Wilson repeat most of what the police had suggested to him, he embellished the story. He told them that on the trip to Saskatoon he noticed Milgaard had a knife. He said that when they had stopped a woman while searching for the Cadrain house, Milgaard had referred to her as a "stupid bitch." He said that after becoming stuck in the snow and he and Milgaard had left John in the car while they went off in different directions to find help. Wilson said that when he returned to the car, he found John hysterical over something she had seen. When Milgaard returned to the car he was out of breath and had blood on his clothes. Wilson added that, on the way to Alberta, Milgaard had thrown a woman's cosmetic case from the car; he also said that, while in Calgary, Milgaard told him he had "got the girl" in Saskatoon. (Karp and Rosner 1991: 63) The police were delighted with the statement. Wilson's story meshed perfectly with Cadrain's. Together they would be a damning indictment against David Milgaard.

Nichol John was subjected to similar treatment. She and Cadrain were placed in a room together and given the opportunity to discuss the events of January 31. Over the next few days she was subjected to many intense interrogation sessions. A heavy drug user, the lonely teenager was terrified and intimidated by the series of events unfolding around her. She told them that she was in full agreement with Cadrain's version of the January events. But she also said more than the police had ever hoped. She said that she saw Milgaard stab Gail Miller. The police now had an eyewitness to the actual murder. David Milgaard was arrested for the murder of Miller and returned to Saskatchewan to stand trial.

THE TRIAL

The two week trial of David Milgaard started in January 1970. As expected, the most damaging testimony came from his friends Cadrain, Wilson and John. Wilson repeated the story he had told the police: how Milgaard had returned to the car out of breath and with blood on his clothes after the two had gone looking for help when the car was stuck in the snow. It was the Crown's contention that, in the fifteen to twenty minute timeframe that they were separated, Milgaard raped and murdered Miller.

At the trial, however, Nichol John presented a problem for the Crown. Having previously told the police that she actually saw Milgaard stab Miller, she then told the court that she could remember nothing of what happened that morning. Not wanting to lose the testimony of the star witness, Crown Prosecutor T.D.R. Caldwell was allowed to treat John as a hostile witness. This would give him the right to cross-examine her and have the previous incriminating statements she gave the police read into the record as evidence against Milgaard.

Cadrain testified, as had Wilson, that he had seen blood on Milgaard's pants the morning of the murder. Certain aspects of Cadrain's testimony had a bizarre quality about them. He said that Milgaard was a member of the Mafia and that he was going to "wipe out" Wilson and John because they knew too much. What the jury and Defence Counsel Calvin Tallis did not know was that Cadrain had claimed the $2,000 reward. He was also was experiencing psychotic delusions in which Milgaard appeared to him in the form of a snake. These episodes prompted Cadrain to enter a psychiatric institute, where he was diagnosed as paranoid schizophrenic.

Although the Crown attempted to bolster its case with non-circumstantial evidence involving blood and antigen identification, the evidence was weak. The defence had done a good job of raising doubt in the minds of the jurors about the reliability of the witnesses' testimony. But Tallis's optimism was shattered by surprising new Crown evidence that suggested that Milgaard had confessed to the murder.

Seventeen-year-old Craig Melnyk and eighteen-year-old George Lapchuk told the court they had been watching a television newscast in a Regina motel room with Milgaard and two girls, Deborah Hall and Ute Frank in May 1969. After watching a story, which said that the police were still looking for Miller's killer, Milgaard was reported to have grabbed a pillow and demonstrated to the group how he had killed the woman, stating several times "I killed her" (Karp and Rosner 1991: 88). Ute Frank was not called by the Crown or the defence, perhaps because she admitted to being very high on drugs and could remember little about the events of that night. For reasons unknown, Deborah Hall was also not called to testify. This oversight would become apparent twenty years later. Melnyk and Lapchuk had a string of previous convictions and in the past had been asked by the police to act as paid informants in drug-related cases. Tallis revealed this past in hopes of discrediting their testimony, but serious damage had been done to Milgaard's defence.

In his instructions to the jury, Justice Alfred Bence was very critical of the Crown's case against David Milgaard. He warned the jury that the testimony of many Crown witnesses should be treated with skepticism. The following day, the jury brought in a guilty verdict. It was exactly one year since Gail Miller's murder.

Bence sentenced Milgaard to life in prison. Tallis prepared an appeal, arguing that Bence had prejudiced the jury by allowing the prosecution to cross-examine John. Serge Kujawa, who had been the chief prosecutor during the trial, was selected to defend the verdict. The Saskatchewan appeal court dismissed the appeal in January 1971. When the Supreme Court of Canada refused to hear the case it appeared that all legal avenues had been exhausted; Milgaard was to spend the rest of his life in jail.

AFTER THE TRIAL

Milgaard's 1979 application for parole was denied because he continued to maintain his innocence and because his early age of imprisonment had not allowed him to mature. However, he was later given escorted leave from the prison for a few hours at a time. During one of these leaves when he was visiting his family in Winnipeg, he slipped away from his escort and made his way to Toronto. He found a job, got a room and a girlfriend and eluded police for seventy-six days. He was considered armed and dangerous by the police. On the seventy-seventh day, his mother, Joyce, was called to Toronto. Her unarmed son, his hands in the air, had been shot in the back by a policeman.

The shooting was not fatal, but it convinced Joyce Milgaard that she had to prove her son's innocence. She offered a $10,000 reward for information leading to the real killer of Gail Miller. With the help of Winnipeg freelance writer Peter Carlyle-Gordge, she started her own investigation of the case. They tracked down Nichol John and Ron Wilson. Wilson hinted that their trial testimony may have been perjured while John said that she had almost no memory of the events of the day of Miller's killing. The Milgaard family also visited the scene of the crime and, with the use of video camera and a stop-watch, determined that Milgaard could not have committed the crime in the timeframe indicated in the court transcripts. Joyce Milgaard also tracked down Deborah Hall, the fifth person in the Regina motel-room party. She said Milgaard had simply been fluffing up a pillow when the news report about Gail Miller was broadcast. One of the other people in the room said to Milgaard, "You did it, didn't you?" According to Hall, all Milgaard said in response was a sarcastic "Oh yeah, right." The family then turned to experienced Winnipeg criminal lawyer Hersh Wolch, who in turn handed the case over to his young associate David Asper. It was Asper's first major case, and he threw himself into the work with considerable enthusiasm.

Dr. James Ferris, a senior forensic pathologist, was commissioned to review the semen and blood samples used against Milgaard at his trial. He concluded that the samples were either contaminated, and therefore should not have been admitted as evidence, or they should have eliminated Milgaard as a suspect. In 1988 Asper and Wolch submitted a request to the justice department for a formal review of the Milgaard case.

While they were awaiting a response to this request, Wolch and Asper received a phone call telling them about a man named Larry Fisher. The caller said that Fisher was then in prison for a series of sexual attacks on women in Saskatoon and Winnipeg. The attacks has taken place about the time of the Miller murder and, most surprising of all, Fisher had been living in the Cadrain house when Gail Miller was murdered. Furthermore, the caller informed them that Fisher's ex-wife Linda had reason to believe that he was the killer. To pursue this new lead Joyce Milgaard turned to Paul Henderson, a Seattle private investigator who specialized in cases of wrongful conviction. With funding from Centurion Ministries, a U.S.-based group dedicated to helping the wrongfully convicted, Henderson found and interviewed Linda Fisher in Cando, Saskatchewan.

She said she believed her ex-husband killed Miller with a paring knife he had taken from their kitchen. He had missed work the day of Miller's murder and had appeared badly shaken when Linda, in a fit of anger, had accused him of killing Miller. Linda Fisher had been surprised to see Henderson because she had given all this information to the police in 1980 after reading of the $10,000 reward being offered by the Milgaard family. She had heard nothing from the police since that time. Henderson then tracked down Ron Wilson. This time Wilson completely recanted the testimony that he gave at the trial. He said that he had been "manipulated by police into lying and later giving false testimony against Milgaard" (Karp and Rosner 1991: 193). Wolch and Asper forwarded the new evidence to Justice Minister Kim Campbell.

Campbell visited Winnipeg several weeks later. The national media followed Campbell's every move during her visit and Joyce Milgaard used the opportunity to confront the Minister while the nation watched. Joyce attempted to hand the Minister a copy of Ferris's blood sample report, but an obviously startled Campbell pushed past her saying, ". . . I'm sorry, but if you want your son to have a fair hearing don't approach me personally" (Karp and Rosner 1991: 216). In February 1991, Campbell made her decision. There would be no review of the David Milgaard case.

But Joyce Milgaard was not about to quit. At her request Henderson interviewed Larry Fisher's rape victims. He discovered that the four women who had been assaulted in Saskatoon had never been informed of Fisher's confessions. From these interviews Henderson learned that the method of attack used by Larry Fisher was similar to that used on Gail Miller. One of the women had already reached the conclusion that it was Fisher, not Milgaard who had murdered Gail Miller. This information, along with the fact that several of Fisher's attacks occurred in the same area as the murder, was sent to Ottawa, to Gail Miller's family and to the media. This was the evidence for which Joyce Milgaard had been hoping. Not only did it point to her son's innocence but it was a strong indication that the police and others in the justice system had repressed evidence that pointed to the real killer. With the resulting publicity came a growing public demand that Milgaard be given a new trial. But she was to receive help from an unexpected source; the prime minister himself would intervene on her behalf.

When Brian Mulroney made a rare visit to Winnipeg in September 1991, Joyce and her supporters waited for him outside his hotel. Mulroney, tipped off that she would be waiting, was careful not to repeat Campbell's mistake. On camera, he approached the group and told Joyce that she was very brave and that he would speak to the justice minister about her son's case. What Mulroney said to Campbell on his return to Ottawa we may never know, but on November 29, 1991, Campbell announced she would ask the Supreme Court of Canada to reopen the case.

THE SUPREME COURT RULING

On April 14, 1992, the Supreme Court brought down its ruling in the David Milgaard case. Interestingly enough, the report began by emphasizing that Milgaard had been given a fair trial in 1970 and there was no evidence of police impropriety in their investigation of the case. However, the court noted that the recantation of Ron Wilson, new evidence regarding the motel room "confession" and the documented activities of serial rapist Larry Fisher constituted credible evidence that could have affected the outcome of the jury's decision in the 1970 trial. The court emphasized that it was not satisfied beyond a reasonable doubt that Milgaard was innocent of the murder, but the new evidence was sufficient to have the guilty verdict quashed and a new trial ordered (*Regina Leader Post*: April 17, 1992). On April 17, 1992, Milgaard was released from prison. He was thirty-nine years old.

Saskatchewan Justice Minister Robert Mitchell decided to stay all charges against Milgaard. He would remain free but there would be no new trial and therefore no opportunity for Milgaard to prove his innocence. Because he was not allowed to prove his innocence, Milgaard's case for compensation for wrongful conviction had been severely weakened. Justifying his decision not to compensate Milgaard, Mitchell stated on April 1, 1991, "We didn't do anything wrong and we take comfort in the fact the Supreme Court agreed with that, so we won't be paying" (*Regina Leader Post:* April 17, 1992).

Joyce Milgaard found evidence indicating that Saskatchewan Premier Roy Romanow, who was justice minister at the time of Milgaard's appeal, and Crown Prosecutor Serge Kujawa had been aware of the similarities between Larry Fisher's crimes and the Miller murder. In response, Mitchell said Joyce Milgaard's charges were unfounded and refused to open an inquiry into the case or consider any compensation for Milgaard. Instead, Mitchell ordered the RCMP to investigate the allegations. The RCMP was instructed to report its findings to the Alberta attorney general's department in order to avoid a conflict of interest (*Regina Leader Post*: November 17, 1992). The RCMP concluded that there had been no wrongdoing on the part of anyone in the Saskatchewan justice department or others involved in Milgaard's arrest and conviction. In 1994 Milgaard sued the Saskatchewan government for wrongful conviction. The following year, after Mitchell told the media that he believed Milgaard was guilty of the murder, Milgaard launched a personal lawsuit against Mitchell.

WHY WAS MILGAARD WRONGFULLY CONVICTED?

The police force, relatively inexperienced with murder cases, responded to public pressure by charging Milgaard for the murder. Milgaard became a suspect when one of his friends pointed the finger at him in an effort to claim the reward money. Aside from Cadrain's evidence and Milgaard's presence in Saskatoon that morning, there was little to link Milgaard to the killing. To build a substantial case against Milgaard the police needed something much more convincing. It was at this stage that they relied on the proven tactics of police coercion and intimidation to extract from Milgaard's companions a statement containing incriminating evidence. These statements were extracted from teenagers: Albert Cadrain, who was emotionally unstable at the time and desperately in need of the reward money; Nichol John, a young insecure woman who was hooked on drugs and terrified by the interrogation procedure; and Ron Wilson, who after many days of police grilling told the police what they wanted to hear just to put an end to his ordeal. Two other teenage witnesses against Milgaard, Craig Melnyk and George Lapchuk, had criminal records of their own. This of course raises the real possibility that the police or prosecution may have made a deal with these witnesses in the form of reduced or dropped charges.

There is also some indication that the police suppressed evidence that would have worked in the interest of David Milgaard. For example, the police knew that several rapes had taken place in Saskatoon and that they were similar to the Miller case. The police did not appear to have followed up on the possibility that the Miller crime and the other rapes were committed by the same person, despite their similarities. Linking the Miller killing to the other crimes would have caused them to suspect that Milgaard may not be the killer: a possibility they apparently did not want to pursue. Nor was it later revealed by the police that Larry Fisher's wife had approached them with the startling story that she believed that her husband had killed Gail Miller and that he was living in the Cadrain house at the time of the murder. There is also evidence of shoddy forensic work on the part of the police, for example, possibly mistaking dog urine for semen samples.

The tumultuous sixties were a time of change and the established social order was under siege. Saskatoon was a small, quiet prairie city in 1969 and murder was a relatively rare event. The city was stunned by the brutal murder, and the atmosphere was charged with a high level of anxiety. The media sensationalized the murder, which exacerbated the public's apprehension. The public demanded that the police apprehend and charge the guilty party.

Once Cadrain drew attention to Milgaard, it appears the police quickly concluded that he was guilty. This was not simply due to Cadrain's evidence or the fact that he was in the area at the time of the murder.

Rather it was because he was a powerless "hippie," living on the fringe of a society that had little use for his kind. Likewise, the intimidation tactics of the police, which forced several young witnesses to give perjured evidence against Milgaard, must be explained within the larger framework of social inequality. Nichol John, Albert Cadrain and Ron Wilson, like Milgaard, were all marginalized from mainstream society and, being vulnerable to police coercion, they quickly succumbed to the pressure. The suppression of evidence must also be regarded within the larger context of social inequality. Police do not suppress evidence in the name of justice; it is done to maintain police power and authority and to insure the vilification of those they have deemed criminal. Police must prove their effectiveness, and the most efficient way of doing this is to ensure that someone is convicted for the crimes that plague society. There would be no cry of protest from the public over Milgaard's arrest, rather all would breathe a sigh of relief that the police had done their job well and the community was again a safe place to live.

David Milgaard became the victim of a justice system gone wrong. He spent twenty-two years in prison for a crime he did not commit because he was a socially marginalized person subject to prejudice, discrimination and community indifference. He was a young man in the wrong place at the wrong time and an easy target for a conservative police force desperately searching for a suspect. Once vilified by the system, the powerful forces of class distinction and social control would work against his claims of innocence. To this day the justice system has never admitted he was wrongfully convicted and continues to block any attempt on his part to prove his innocence.

AFTERWORD

In the summer of 1997 DNA testing, conducted at the Milgaard family's initiative, provided positive proof of David Milgaard's innocence. It was only at this point that the Saskatchewan government announced its intent to compensate Milgaard and to launch a public inquiry into his conviction. In July 1997 the police arrested Larry Miller and charged him with the murder of Gail Miller.

NOTE

1.   For a detailed account of this case see Karp and Rosner 1991; Hughes 1992; and Jenish 1992.

4

The Case
of Wilbert Coffin

THE DEFENDANT

Wilbert Coffin was a forty-two-year-old uneducated prospector and
woodsman. He lived in the small Quebec town of York Centre and
worked in the wilderness area of Quebec's Gaspé peninsula. He was
an English-speaking Protestant in a predominantly French-speaking
Roman Catholic community. Coffin was well-liked by most people
who came to know him, but his poverty, religion, poor education and
language made Wilbert Coffin visible and vulnerable with respect to
mainstream Quebec society.[1]

THE CRIME

Even today the rugged wilderness of Quebec's Gaspé peninsula
attracts tourists from around the world. But in 1953 the attraction of
this region was not only its wild beauty but also its black bear
population. The hundreds of American hunters who trekked annually
to the Gaspé, in search of the elusive animal, were a mainstay of the
region's economy.

On June 5, 1953, Eugene Lindsey, his seventeen-year-old son
Richard and their nineteen-year-old friend Frederick Claar left their
home in Pennsylvania for a three-week hunting adventure in the
Gaspé bush. On June 8 the three arrived in the small town of Gaspé
where they purchased supplies. The hunters had been expected back
in Pennsylvania about the middle of June. When they had not arrived
by July 5, Claar's father contacted the Quebec Provincial Police. It
took an additional call from the Pennsylvania police before the
Quebec police organized a search. Their truck was found on July 10.
Near the truck the searchers found a crumpled and weathered note
written by one of the hunters. Dated June 13, 1953, the note suggests
that the men had split up at some point and one of them had left the

note for the others, saying he had returned to the truck and was leaving again. This note was never presented at the trial, and a subsequent government commission of inquiry rejected the note's existence. The bodies and belongings of the three men were found about five miles from their truck.

So badly were the bodies mauled and the clothing torn that experts first thought the men had been killed by bears. Only later did they discover a bullet mark on Richard Lindsey's tattered shirt. The rifle stock found near Eugene Lindsey's skull fragment had been damaged by a bullet and human hairs were found embedded in the stock's butt end. Police speculated that in a struggle with his assailant Eugene Lindsey had been knocked out by a blow to the head from the rifle butt. This would also explain how a section of his skull had been dislodged. A number of the hunters' personal items were found strewn along a bush trail near where the bodies had been found. Many of these items were hanging from tree branches and bushes as if they had been thrown from a moving vehicle. Eugene Lindsey was known to carry large sums of money with him; his empty wallet was found along the bank of the river near his body.

The discovery of the bodies made headlines in the United States. The government of Quebec Premier Maurice Duplessis was soon under pressure from a variety of sources, including the American State Department, to find and prosecute the killer. Clearly any murder that involved the American State Department and threatened the lucrative tourist industry of Quebec was no ordinary crime. Duplessis intended to appease the Americans as quickly as possible.

When the call went out for volunteers to help search for the three Americans, Wilbert Coffin offered his services. He told the police that he had assisted the three Americans in the bush when the fuel pump on their truck developed a problem. In the minds of the police Coffin was probably the last person to see the three men alive. As a result he was detained as a material witness in the case. A short time later he was arrested and charged with the murder of Eugene Lindsey.

Responsibility for investigating the case and gathering evidence against Coffin was given to Captain Alphonse Matte of the Quebec Provincial Police. Matte had a reputation as a hard-nosed cop. Even before he had any real evidence, he was convinced that Coffin was guilty. Duplessis handed the prosecution of the case to Paul Miquelon and Noel Dorion, two of Quebec's best-known prosecutors. Between them, they had secured an impressive number of convictions.

Coffin's brother retained Alphonse Garneau to act as Wilbert's defence counsel. In a letter to Coffin, Garneau warned him to say nothing to the police without counsel present. He had sent the letter to Coffin through Captain Matte who in turn gave it to Duplessis, who was the province's attorney general as well the premier. Coffin never received the message and talked openly when interrogated by Matte.

However, Garneau's career as Coffin's lawyer was to be short-lived. An attorney by the name of Raymond Maher presented himself to Coffin's father as one of Quebec's best defence lawyers. He convinced the father that Coffin's only chance was to hire him. On his father's advice, Coffin dismissed Garneau and hired Maher. In retrospect, this act may have cost Coffin his life.

THE TRIAL

Throughout the trial the prosecution's argument was that Coffin killed the three American hunters and then robbed them. The evidence for this claim was that Coffin had been seen spending a substantial amount of money—including some American money—after the murders. Eugene Lindsey was known to carry such sums of money on his person and his empty wallet had been found at the crime scene. At the time of his arrest Coffin had in his possession a valise, an automobile fuel pump, a pocket knife and a pair of binoculars, all of which belonged to the murdered hunters.

Although the murder weapon was never found, the prosecution attempted to imprint an image of the weapon and its disappearance in the minds of the jury. It argued that Coffin had borrowed a rifle in early May 1953 and never returned it. The prosecution said that Coffin had used this borrowed rifle to kill the three Americans and then hid it near his camp. It further suggested Coffin had then asked his brother Donald to retrieve the rifle for him. The prosecution presented evidence that a vehicle had been heard in the vicinity of the gate leading to Coffin's camp. The police found truck tire marks in the mud going around the gate. However, a police search of Coffin's camp and the surrounding area did not locate the rifle (Hebert 1964). The prosecution suggested that the driver of the vehicle heard in the vicinity of the gate had been Coffin's brother on his way to the camp to pick up the rifle. This evidence was pure speculation and should have been disallowed by the presiding judge.

Witness Wilson McGregor testified that he had seen the tip of a rifle in the back of Coffin's panel truck shortly after the crime had been committed. Overlooked was the fact that it was twilight when McGregor supposedly saw the rifle in the truck and that he had been standing about twenty-five metres from the truck at the time of the sighting. One wonders why the defence did not question how the rifle could have been picked up from Coffin's camp and hidden by his brother at the same time that it was seen in the back of Wilbert Coffin's truck. It also seems incredible to suggest that a man would kill three people and then display the weapon so openly. Nonetheless, this was the uncontested evidence presented at the trial and it was to play a major part in Coffin's conviction.

One year after the trial Wilson McGregor clarified his trial testimony in a sworn statement filed with the justice minister. In the statement he claimed he had seen equipment, including pots and pans, in the back of Coffin's truck, along with what he took to be the barrel of a rifle. He states, "[I]t could have been a rod of iron. I never saw a hole in the end of this rod of iron nor did I see the trigger or the stock of any rifle" (Hebert 1964: 155). McGregor also stated that while the records show that he said he saw the rifle on June 12, it could have been any time during the second week in June.

The prosecution's case was based entirely on circumstantial evidence. Coffin had freely admitted that he had met the three Americans in the bush. When first interrogated he said that the Americans told him their truck was not working because of a faulty fuel pump. Coffin said he drove the younger Lindsey back to Gaspé to buy a new pump and then returned him to the camp. However, the prosecution contended that when the American's truck was later examined it was found to be in working order and the pump had not been changed. Coffin, it was argued, had fabricated the fuel pump story. Coffin's possession of the Americans' valise, fuel pump, binoculars and a pocket knife was also entered as evidence.

While this evidence may demonstrate that Coffin was a petty thief and may have been in possession of a gun, it did not prove he was a killer. But Miquelon used his considerable oratorical skills to convince the jury of Coffin's guilt. Miquelon painted Coffin as a dangerous and skilled predator, a hunter of men. The members of the jury were enraptured by the performance, but not convinced. They remembered Maher's public comment that he would put one hundred witnesses on the stand that would prove Coffin innocent. When the prosecution concluded its case, all eyes in the courtroom turned on Raymond Maher as he stood to begin his defence. Maher remained silent for a few seconds as he faced the judge. The few words he finally spoke to the court effectively sealed the fate of his client. "My Lord, the Defence rests" (Hebert 1964: 66).

All the promised witnesses had been little more than a publicity stunt. Maher had secured no witnesses; it is questionable if he had even attempted to do so. The man who had presented himself to Coffin's father as one of Quebec's greatest lawyers had done virtually nothing for his client. Furthermore, he had even refused to let Coffin testify in his own defence. Hearing only the prosecution's dramatic interpretation of the events, the jury had little choice but to find Coffin guilty of first degree murder.

He was sentenced to be hanged in Quebec's Bordeaux Jail on August 5, 1954. Several appeals were launched but these did little more than delay the inevitable. On February 10, 1956, forty-four-year-old Wilbert Coffin was hung by the neck until dead. He proclaimed his innocence to the end.

THE SEARCH FOR TRUTH: COFFIN'S STORY

Although never allowed to testify at his trial, Coffin did leave behind a statement rebutting the Crown's case against him. Coffin contends that on June 10 he came across the three Americans in the bush and drove Richard Lindsey back to Gaspé to secure a new fuel pump. On the return trip the youth had given him the knife as a token of thanks. When they returned to the American's camp Eugene Lindsey and Frederick Claar were in the company of two other men. Coffin claims that these men were introduced to him as two Americans who were also bear hunting. The two men were driving a jeep with a foreign license plate. The vehicle had been closed in with plywood, which was stained or painted yellow.

After having a late meal with the five Americans, Coffin claims he left them, promising to return in two days to see if they were having any trouble. He returned to the location on June 12 as promised. The Lindsey's truck had not been moved, but there was no sign of the yellow jeep. He assumed that the Lindseys were somewhere in the bush. He decided to wait for them and consumed a considerable amount of alcohol over a two-hour period. His inhibitions dulled by the alcohol, he rummaged through their truck and took the valise, binoculars and fuel pump before returning to Gaspé. On his arrival back in Gaspé that day he decided he would visit his common-law wife in Montreal.

Coffin denied ever having a gun in his truck at this time. However, he was carrying considerable camping equipment in the truck, any item of which could have been mistaken for the barrel of a rifle in the subdued light of the late evening. As noted previously, McGregor himself later filed a statement indicating that what he took to be a gun in Coffin's truck could have been a rod of iron.

As for the money in his possession after the murders, Coffin painstakingly documented its source. He supplied a list of people he had collected money from before and after the murders as payment to him for staking mining claims and other services rendered.

WHY WAS COFFIN WRONGFULLY CONVICTED?

Hebert argues that Wilbert Coffin was the victim of a system controlled by corrupt politicians and an obedient state police that was willing to sustain and service that corruption. When the American hunters were found murdered, the Duplessis government was pressured by the 200,000-member Pennsylvania Federation of Sportman's Clubs. This organization received political support from Congressman James E. VanZant, who urged the State Department to pressure the Quebec government to apprehend a suspect in the case. Hebert (1964) suggests that the Duplessis administration was therefore in desperate need of a villain to present before the Americans as proof that Quebec was again a safe and secure haven for tourism. Wilbert Coffin had been in the area about the time of the murders. More importantly, he was poor, non-Catholic, uneducated and spoke no French. From the police point of view Wilbert Coffin was both vulnerable and available. Once he was targeted all evidence pointing to other suspects would be either ignored or suppressed by the police and the prosecution.

Shortly after Coffin had been apprehended, his original lawyer, Alphonse Garneau, sent via the attorney general's office the afore-mentioned telegram warning Coffin not to make any statement to the police until he was in the presence of counsel. The telegram had been delivered personally to Duplessis but it never reached Coffin. The suppressed telegram meant Coffin was unaware of his rights when he was interrogated by the police and this probably compromised his defence.

A note dated June 13 and signed by one of the murdered men presented clear evidence that the hunters were still alive after Coffin had left the area for Montreal. This note disappeared before the trial and never became part of the evidence supporting Coffin's innocence. In 1963 Jacques Hebert interviewed Lewis Synnett, a former Quebec Provincial Police officer who had worked on the Coffin investigation. Synnett stated in the presence of several witnesses that he " was in Captain Matte's office with some other people. . . . I saw on his desk the first note; the one showing at least one of the hunters was alive on June 13" (Hebert 1964: 44).

In a later interview with Jacques Hebert, *Toronto Daily Star* reporter John Edward Belliveau, who covered the Coffin case, stated that the note was "signed by one of the three hunters, bearing a date, it was proof that the signatory was living on June 13th, being a day following Coffin's departure" (Hebert 1964: 43). If these statements are to be believed, it appears that the police simply suppressed this evidence in order to sustain their case against Coffin.

The personal articles belonging to the victims that had been found by the police were hanging from branches along the road as if they had been hurled from a fast moving vehicle. This suggests that a driver and at least one other person may have been in the vehicle at the time. Because they were claiming Coffin acted alone in the murder, the police down played this evidence as immaterial.

Many persons swore under oath to seeing in the area a jeep with Pennsylvania license plates being driven by two young men at the time of the murders. The witnesses' description of this vehicle and its occupants was identical to Coffin's description of the hunters and the vehicle he saw with the Lindseys on June 12. Alwin Tapp, a member of the Moncton police department, and his brother Gerald reported speaking to an American hunter in Gaspé on June 17. The man, who drove a jeep with yellow plywood siding, said he was waiting for a guide to take him into the bush. A Dr. Wilson and his wife swore they saw a jeep with wood siding and Pennsylvania plates in the area on June 9. The jeep was being driven by two men who were about thirty-years-old and wearing American Army jackets.

Some of the witnesses stated that the two men in the jeep had made inquiries about the whereabouts of the Lindsey hunting party. The police sought out Dr. Gordon Burkett and Charles E. Ford of Pennsylvania. These men had traveled to the Gaspé in a jeep but had left the region before the crime. The fact that these two men drove a jeep to the Gaspé did not account for the many sightings of a wood-covered jeep after their departure. However, this was the only explanation offered by the police and the prosecution for the various jeep sightings.

Jacques Hebert (1964) states that the police made no real effort to find this vehicle and its occupants because if they had been successful the case against Coffin would have fallen apart. Furthermore, had it been discovered that the hunters had been murdered by fellow Americans the political consequences of trying Americans in a Canadian court would have had a profoundly negative effect on the American tourist trade in the Gaspé—the very condition that Duplessis was trying to avoid. It was necessary that the killer be a Canadian.

We will never know why Coffin's lawyer, Raymond Maher, presented virtually no defence. Perhaps he believed no defence was necessary because the Crown had not proven its case. On the other hand there is the possibility that Maher was so incompetent that he did not know how to muster a defence. During the trial, Maher informed the court he was leaving for a few days to talk to over fifty people who would testify on behalf of his client. The jury was left with the impression that Coffin obviously had a strong defence. When Maher refused to allow Coffin to testify on his own behalf and never produced the promised witnesses, the jury concluded that the prospector must be guilty. Had Coffin been given the opportunity to counter the prosecution's claims and present his testimony the jury might have found him not guilty. The fact he was denied this opportunity may itself be considered a miscarriage of justice.

The prosecution's actions throughout the trial were far from exemplary. Marion Petrie, Coffin's common-law wife, was summoned as a Crown witness. However, she presented testimony that Coffin had informed her about the two Americans in the yellow jeep even before he was a suspect in the case. In a frantic effort at damage control the Crown took the questionable step of cross-examining its own witness in an attempt to discredit her testimony.

It should also be remembered that the police had never found the murder weapon. Nonetheless, the prosecution fabricated a weapon in the minds of the jury by insinuating that a rifle had been spirited away from Coffin's camp by his brother or another sympathizer. Because there was no evidence to support this suggestion it was little more than speculation and should never have been considered by the court (Hebert 1964).

The Coffin case is particularly disconcerting because it illuminates the fact that if economic and political conditions demand, the state may be prepared to vilify its own citizens under the guise of justice. The case is also compelling because it highlights the killing of innocent people by the state in the name of justice. The horror is much sharper if it can be demonstrated that the state authorities proceeded to execution with full knowledge that the accused was innocent.

The Wilbert Coffin case forces all thinking people to consider how many others who suffered the penalty of death in Canada were victims of an unjust system. One also wonders what might have been the fate of Donald Marshall, David Milgaard, Guy Paul Morin, Steven Truscott, Thomas Sophonow and the countless others who were wrongfully convicted if Canada had retained and exercised the death penalty. The thought is sobering.

NOTE

1. Information in this chapter was derived from Hebert 1964 and Capital Case Files 1956.

5

The Case of Guy Paul Morin

THE DEFENDANT

Guy Paul Morin was marginalized from the community in which he lived. Indeed, in terms of small-town standards of behaviour, the entire Morin family was unusual. This family displayed unbridled affection for one another in ways that some people found embarrassing; a family that set up floodlights in their backyard so they could tinker with old cars well into the wee hours of the morning, even when others in the community were out searching for a missing little girl. The interior of the house could politely be described as messy, with clothes, books, furniture, boxes and equipment scattered around the rooms in a careless disregard for neatness and order. The family seemed to exclude the community from their lives and was almost fanatical about their privacy. Guy Paul Morin was himself unusual. A young man in his early twenties who was still living with his parents and who seldom dated girls, preferring instead the company of his honey bees. A skilled musician, he could lose himself in his music and loved to play the tunes of Benny Goodman and the Big Band era. He had a strange cadence to his speech pattern and often chose inappropriate words to express himself. It was this combination of characteristics that would cause the police investigators to regard him as "weird."[1]

THE CRIME

Queensville is a typical, small bedroom community located about sixty kilometres north of Toronto. Living next door to each other in this village were two people who would become major players in one of Canada's most highly publicized murder cases; nine-year-old Christine Jessop and twenty-four-year-old Guy Paul Morin.

On Wednesday, October 3, 1984, Christine Jessop stepped off the school bus in front of her home, clutching the new recorder that she and other students had been given that day. It was 3:45 in the afternoon. When she entered the house she was not surprised to find it empty. Her mother Janet had told Christine that morning that she would be late arriving home because she had some business to attend to in town.

Christine Jessop then rode her bike to meet her friend Leslie Chipman in the park. On the way she stopped at the local store to buy some gum and had a brief conversation with the store owner. After leaving the store she was spotted by Robert Atkinson talking to three young friends. She was still clutching her new recorder. When fifteen-year-old Kim Warren left the store shortly after Christine, she glanced down the street and noticed Christine walking her bicycle up the driveway of the Jessop home. Christine Jessop did not keep her appointment in the park with her friend. In fact, she was never seen alive again.

Almost the entire community became involved in the search for the little girl, but there were few leads to follow. As hours became days and days dragged into weeks, it became more and more apparent to the York Regional Police that Christine Jessop was probably dead. Because she was last seen entering the house the police assumed that she had been abducted by someone who was waiting for her to arrive home. On New Year's Eve, 1984, eighty-nine days after she disappeared, her badly decomposed body was found by Fred Patterson in a bush near his home fifty kilometres from Queensville. An autopsy revealed that she had been raped and mutilated.

After Christine Jessop's abduction and the subsequent discovery of her decomposed body the community of Queensville and the surrounding region was in a state of disbelief and shock. A sexually motivated killing and mutilation of a child is considered one of the most heinous of human acts, regardless of where it happens. When it occurs in a sleepy rural village the effect on the community is horrendous. Early in the investigation the people of Queensville realized that the abductor was probably a member of the community, perhaps their next-door neighbour. The unceasing police activity and the presence of the national media in the village nurtured a suspicion among the people toward one another that bordered on paranoia. Furthering this community anxiety was a festering belief that the police were conducting an incompetent investigation. The police were not immune to the rancour of the citizens and, when this was combined with attention focused on them by the national media, they felt the pressure to produce a suspect.

THE INVESTIGATION

The location of the body thrust the case into the hands of the Durham Regional Police. Detectives Bernie Fitzpatrick and John Shephard took charge of the investigation. The first snowfall of the year threatened to obscure any evidence that may have existed at the body site. Knowing it would be impossible to look for evidence after heavy snow, the police searched the location throughout the night and located Jessop's recorder along with a few buttons and other small bits of possible evidence near the body. Several hours after its discovery, her dismembered skeletal remains were removed to the coroner's office in Toronto.

As an example of police investigative techniques, the search of the body site can only be described as a fiasco. As journalist Kirk Makin (1995) notes, for any homicide investigation the preservation of the crime scene is of the utmost importance. The first consideration after the discovery of the body should have been to secure the crime site and cover it with a large tent. This would have allowed the police and forensic experts to conduct a standardized grid search of the area and to collect soil and other organic samples from around the body. Such samples could have assisted in estimating how long the body had been at the location and if the murder had taken place at the body site. The rather primitive and shoddy investigative techniques employed by the police would later raise serious questions about police reliability throughout the entire investigation.

The search for the killer would prove to be a tremendous challenge for a small rural police force with limited experience in homicide cases. Many Queensville residents were interviewed, as were people living near the body site. Lydia Robertson, who lived with her son near-by, told Fitzpatrick and Shephard that on the night of the murder she had heard what she thought was a child screaming for help. She had concluded that the screams had come from quarrelling neighbours. Other people living in the area also claimed to have heard cries for help that same night. The detectives later concluded that Robertson could not have heard screams from the body site after they had a child cry for help while they listened from Robertson's house. This experiment, however, was conducted during the peak of rush hour traffic on the nearby highway.

The autopsy revealed some interesting evidence that added to police frustration. An analysis of Jessop's bone marrow indicated the same results as found in victims of drowning. The pink colour of her teeth also indicated drowning. This particular discovery was never pursued by the police, who preferred to believe, as the coroner had suggested, that these results may have been caused by contaminated samples. It was also noted that, while Jessop had suffered two sharp blows to the head, these blows were probably not the cause of death. Judging from two knife wounds on what was left of the skin on the torso and the several cuts in her clothing, it was thought that death had been caused by wounds. A single dark hair, not consistent with her hair type, was removed from the necklace she had been wearing. The buttons found at the body site were different from those that had been ripped from her blouse. Adding to the confusion was the fact that the sweater found with the body was one that the Jessops did not recognize. There was also the question of why the body was still clothed in underwear on which semen stains had been discovered. This fact suggested that the panties had been replaced after the sexual assault had taken place at another location. It appears, however, that the police gave low priority to the possibility that Jessop was assaulted before being driven to the body site.

Six weeks later Fitzpatrick and Shephard felt they were no closer to finding the killer. However, in the course of interviewing the Jessops, Fitzpatrick made an entry in his notebook regarding the young man who lived with his parents next door: "Guy Paul Morin, clarinet player, weird type guy" (Makin 1992: 98).

Fitzpatrick and Shephard invited Morin out to their car for a talk, which they intended to secretly record. For some unexplained reason, the tape recorder stopped before the end of the interview. Nonetheless, Fitzpatrick and Shephard claim that during the untaped part of the interview Morin made the comment that "innocent little girls grow up to be corrupt" (Makin 1992: 142). This comment was sufficient for Fitzpatrick and Shephard to conclude that Morin should be considered a key suspect in the killing of Christine Jessop.

The tunnel vision that caused the police to concentrate on Morin does not mean that there were no other suspects. Kirk Makin (1992) states that several suspects (all of whom were marginalized people) were known to the police but were never investigated thoroughly. (For legal reasons, the names he uses for these suspects are pseudo-nyms and will be used here.) Makin relates how Gabriel Polgar, who lived near the body site, informed the police that he had seen a parked car near the site shortly after Jessop's abduction. The trunk of the car was up but there was no one in or around the vehicle. Stopping to investigate he heard someone in the nearby bush making a noise that sounded like leaves being kicked. A short time later a large man rushed from the bush breathing heavily. Startled by Polgar's presence the man glared at him menacingly, slammed the trunk closed and quickly drove off. Apparently, the police made no attempt to follow up on Polgar's story.

Another possible suspect was a young man called Dean MacPhail. An employee at the Queensville cemetery next to Christine's house, he had a history of sexual misconduct. His teachers believed that he was dangerous to the point of being homicidal. He was checked out by the police but his family claimed he had been with them at the time of the abduction. This alibi was weak at best, and in 1989 MacPhail's sister confided to a friend that the family had covered for him; he had not been with them when Christine went missing.

Brad Foster was perhaps the most obvious of all the suspects. The York Regional Police investigated him after a concerned social worker drew him to their attention. According to Makin (1992), Foster was a huge seventeen-year-old orphan who had bounced from one group home to another and had been convicted of numerous petty crimes. In 1983 he was ejected from yet another group home not far from the body site after he was discovered having sex with several young children in the home. He drifted around the area until he came under the care of a kindly social worker, who brought him into his own home. Foster soon got a job with a car dealership, delivering parts around the region in an old van. His job would have allowed him to become familiar with all the back roads in the region, including the body site. After a few weeks the social worker believed Foster to be a deeply troubled and dangerous young man. Suddenly, in early October 1994, Foster disappeared from the home and did not show up for work. When the social worker heard of Jessop's disappearance he informed Durham police of his suspicions.

Checking the car dealership where Foster had worked, they discovered that he had disappeared shortly after having an accident with the company van. The police noted the broken windows in the van and concluded that the interior had been exposed to the elements for so long that forensic analysis would be futile. The police did not investigate further. Much later the defence team heard of Foster and hired a private detective, Basil Mangano, to trace Foster and determine his activities on October 4, 1984.

Foster's employer told Mangano that on the day Jessop was abducted, Foster was to deliver parts to Mississauga and that the delivery was never made. Confronted by his employer, Foster said he had gone to Sharon to visit friends. Gas receipts signed by Foster substantiated his claim. What the employer found most peculiar was that, the morning after the abduction, Foster had washed the old van inside and out with powerful industrial detergent, going so far as to carefully scrub the seats and dashboard. Foster had never washed the van before. In fact, as a utility vehicle covered with grease from old auto parts, it was beyond cleaning. On November 26, 1984, Foster smashed the van. His employer was furious to learn that Foster had not reported the accident and immediately called the police. He was told the police would arrive the following morning to investigate. When the police arrived Foster had disappeared and he was never seen again by his employer. He was in such a hurry to leave town that he did not even bother to pick up his final paycheck. Mangano finally tracked him down in a Toronto rooming house, at which time he denied any involvement with the crime. The police did not bother to pursue that matter.

A fourth possible suspect in the case was sixteen-year-old Bill Larocque. Ben Jarvenpaa, a social worker, knew Larocque to be a potentially dangerous young man. Jarvenpaa contacted the Durham police shortly after the discovery of Jessop's body and told them that Larocque was sexually aggressive, carried a knife and had been arrested for several crimes. After forcing sex on a twelve-year-old girl in one of the group homes in which he was living, Larocque was relocated to a group home in Queensville in the summer of 1984. He roamed the Queensville region and would have been familiar with the body site area. The police did not concentrate on Laroque when the group home log book showed he had been home at the time of Christine's disappearance. Instead, they pursued Morin.

But there was a major problem in the case against Morin. On October 3, Janet Jessop and her son Kenny had made a visit to the dentist and done some shopping. They told the police that they had returned home at 4:10 p.m. The records indicated that Guy Paul Morin had left his place of work in Toronto at 3:32. Considering the traffic at that time of day he could not have arrived back home in Queensville before 4:15. Obviously, if Christine was not home at 4:10, as her mother claimed, it would have been impossible for Morin to have abducted her. If Morin was to remain a police suspect, it was imperative that Mrs. Jessop reconsider her time of arrival. After a meeting with Fitzpatrick and Sheppard, Janet Jessop did just that. She now claimed that she and Kenny returned to the house sometime between 4:30 and 4:40, a timeframe that allowed Morin to be at the Jessop residence when Christine arrived home from school. However, even with this window of opportunity, the police had nothing but the flimsiest of circumstantial evidence against Morin. He lived next door to the victim, she had a new recorder and he was a clarinet player, he had a "weird personality" and he had opportunity. Morin had absolutely no history of trouble with the law and he seldom spoke to Christine. What was needed was hard physical evidence linking Morin with Christine Jessop. For this they turned to the forensic experts.

The coroner had found one black hair entwined in Jessop's necklace that was inconsistent with the victim's hair type. Could this hair be from Guy Paul Morin? The police needed a hair sample from Morin but, because they didn't want to spook him into flight, it would be necessary to get the sample without making him aware that he was a suspect. Posing as a student hairdresser and a friend of a fellow musician, an undercover police woman attended a band practice and asked several members of the band for hair samples. Morin agreed to her request and she snipped a small sample of his hair and placed it in an envelope. Subsequent laboratory examination of the hair indicated it was similar to the type found in the necklace. It is important to note that hair analysis is not a perfect science. A forensic expert can never say that two hairs are a "match," but it can be stated that two or more hairs have similar characteristics. Nonetheless, the analysis was all that was needed to convince the police that Guy Paul Morin had raped, mutilated and killed Christine Jessop. No motive for the killing was needed.

The police developed the theory that when Christine Jessop arrived home she was disappointed because there was no one to whom she could show off her new recorder. Remembering that Guy Paul Morin was a musician, she sought him out. This gave him the chance for which he had long been waiting. He abducted her, took her to a remote location and raped her. He probably had not intended to kill her, but when she resisted his advances he went into a blind rage, killing her and dismembering her body. The police further postulated that Morin possibly had a dual personality and was not even aware that he had killed the girl. It was around this theory that they attempted to fit the various pieces of circumstantial evidence.

Fitzpatrick and Shephard reasoned that if Morin was the killer, he would have transported Jessop to the body site in his Honda. They obtained a warrant to search the vehicle hoping to find fibres from Jessop's clothing. After acquiring a key for his car from the local Honda dealer and completing a series of tapings to lift fibre material from the seats, floor and trunk of the vehicle, they turned these fibres over to the same laboratory that had done the hair analysis. The Durham police also requested help from the U.S.A. National Center for the Analysis of Violent Crime, a branch of the Federal Bureau of Investigation (FBI). This center had recently developed a new technique of creating a killer's psychological profile by analyzing all the evidence pertinent to a case.

Fitzpatrick and Shephard shipped the relevant material to the center, asking if it would be possible to prepare a profile of Christine's killer. The FBI was sufficiently interested to send Agent John Douglas to Ontario to more closely examine the body site and other evidence. Douglas prepared a psychological profile of the killer which noted, among other things, that Christine's killer was young and probably lived near the victim. He was a night-owl and solitary in nature, and he was familiar with the area where the body was discovered. The profile was an almost perfect description of Guy Paul Morin. Certainly Morin would have some knowledge of the area around the body site because he had at one time kept several hives of bees in the region. Douglas had also advised them on how to proceed with the investigation including the interrogation of the suspect. The walls of the interrogation room should be decorated with various props such as enlarged fingerprints and eye-catching photographs of various pieces of physical evidence such as Christine's clothing and recorder. The purpose of this charade was to convince the suspect that a special task force working on the case was in possession of sufficient evidence to secure a conviction.

THE ARREST AND TRIAL

The FBI profile was all Fitzpatrick and Shephard needed to arrest Morin for murder. On April 22, 1985, as he was driving to band practice, Morin noticed the flashing red lights of a police cruiser in his rearview mirror. As the officers approached his car, Morin recognized them as the friendly cops he had recently chatted with at his home. He was shocked beyond belief when they handcuffed him, told him he was under arrest for the first degree murder of Christine Jessop and whisked him off to the Whitby police station. He was led into a small interrogation room that had been prepared in the way suggested by FBI Agent Douglas. Morin was interrogated for several hours by Fitzpatrick and Sheppard, who informed him that the blow-up of the fingerprint on the wall had been lifted from Christine's clothes and that it was his. The fingerprint was indeed Morin's, but it was from Morin's clarinet. But Morin was not acting like a guilt-ridden killer. He remained calm and insisted that he had never touched the girl and could offer no explanation for the fingerprint being on her clothing.

While Morin was undergoing interrogation, police officers in Queensville had secured a warrant to search the Morin home. About a dozen officers combed the house for twelve hours and took away several large boxes of clothing and other personal effects. Some-where in this gathered material they hoped to find evidence against Morin but, as they were to discover later, there was nothing that would implicate him. Furthermore, Stephanie Nyznyk, the labora-tory worker who had analyzed the hair sample taken from Morin, now informed the police that none of the hundreds of the foreign fibres found on Christine's clothing were similar to the upholstery material in Morin's car. She also noted that most of the foreign fibres found on Jessop were red wool, and none of these had been found in Morin's Honda. In fact, the only positive thing that Nyznyk could offer the detectives was that both the Honda and the clothing had revealed five similar foreign fibres. This was not a surprising discov-ery, given the fact that the Morins and Jessops were next door neighbours and both used a common laundromat. The five consistent fibres were not the kind of evidence that should have been entered in court.

The police continued trying to extract a confession from Morin at the Whitby jail. One day Morin was moved to a cell occupied by

Gordon Hobbs, a member of the Toronto police force who was posing as an inmate. The cell had been wired so that any conversation would be recorded. During the three days the men shared a cell, Hobbs tried to get Morin to talk about the murder and his relationship with Jessop. The resulting tapes were of very poor quality but the police were satisfied that the exercise had been productive. They were particularly intrigued with a section of the tape that had Morin describing one of his favourite movies, *The Shining*. Morin spoke of a scene in which one of the characters repeats the words Redrum, Redrum, over and over. Morin had explained that Redrum was "murder" spelled backward. Morin had also stated on the tape that no one would ever know the real relationship he had with Christine Jessop. Fitzpatrick and Shephard felt that in the hands of a skilled prosecutor these segments of the tape could be powerful evidence against Morin.

A short time later Shephard received word that two inmates at Whitby jail wanted to talk with him about Morin. One of the most common techniques used by the police when they have very little hard evidence against a suspect is to make deals with prison inmates, who then gather evidence for them. The reasoning behind this practice is the notion that a suspect being held in jail will be open and frank with a fellow convict, even to the point of bragging about the crimes he or she has committed. The men who called Shephard to the Whitby jail were Robert May and a man who can be identified only as Mr. X. Both these men had notorious reputations. May had assaulted a guard at the Whitby jail, forged cheques, engaged in fraud and was an admitted chronic liar. Mr. X could best be described as a weak man on the verge of a nervous breakdown. May tried to protect Mr. X from the usual prison bullies and in return Mr. X would do almost anything May asked of him, including fabricate evidence. Many years as a petty criminal had taught May how to work the justice system to his own advantage. May told Shephard that in exchange for a lesser sentence he would testify that Morin had admitted to the killing. Furthermore, Mr. X would corroborate Morin's confession. Shephard made a deal with the men to have their sentences reduced if they could get Morin to repeat the confession on tape. The men were wired and placed in a cell with Morin. They were unsuccessful in getting an incriminating statement on tape but agreed to swear in court that Morin had confessed to them about the murder.

Meanwhile, Morin and his family had replaced their first lawyer with Clayton Ruby, a Toronto lawyer who had made a name for himself defending and winning tough, high-profile cases. Ruby did not believe the prosecution had a good case against his client but as an experienced lawyer he knew there was always the possibility of a conviction regardless of the evidence. He wanted a back-up position that insured Morin would never go to the penitentiary even if found guilty. Ruby intended to ask for a "bifurcated" trial. In essence, this would mean a two-part trial in which the jury would first be required to decide if Morin had killed Jessop. If they concluded he did, then the trial would move to the second stage in which the jury would decide if he had committed the act with willful intent. It is within this second stage that the legal question of insanity is considered. However, if Morin was found not guilty during the first stage the second stage is dropped and the question of insanity never surfaces. In preparation Ruby had a number of psychologists evaluate Morin. Two concluded that Morin was a schizophrenic who, under stressful conditions, was capable of doing almost anything. The source of Morin's problem was thought to be the family situation in which he had been raised. Another psychologist concluded that he was not schizophrenic.

Ruby requested a change of venue for the trial, arguing that Morin could not receive a fair hearing in the emotionally charged counties of York or Durham. The judge moved the trial to London, Ontario. The presiding judge would be Archibald McLeod Craig and the prosecution team would be led by John Scott. Much of the evidence presented to the jury at the trial was highly circumstantial and the fibre and hair evidence extremely tenuous. Ruby destroyed the "jailhouse confession" testimony presented by Mr. X. and Robert May. Morin's best defence was the time factor. The Crown asserted that on October 3, 1983 Morin left work and arrived in Queensville at 4:15 p.m., immediately snatched Jessop from her home, drove fifty kilometres to the body site, raped and dismembered the body, drove back to Queensville, destroyed his blood-stained clothes and cleaned the blood from his body and car before appearing at his house with groceries at 5:30. The Crown was asking the jury to believe that Morin had done all this driving, raping, killing, cleaning and shopping in seventy-five minutes.

The judge refused to grant a bifurcated trial. Ruby told the Morins he would drop the case if he was not allowed to introduce the evidence of the psychologists who believed that Morin was a schizophrenic. This would have allowed the jury to acquit him on the grounds of insanity if it concluded he was guilty. Morin reluctantly approved the strategy. He and his family, however, never accepted the diagnosis.

The jury deliberated thirteen hours before filing back into the courtroom and presenting a verdict of not guilty. Ruby held his breath, expecting the jury foreman to add the words "by reason of insanity," but the foreman seated himself and said no more. Kenny Jessop screamed in disbelief and hammered the bench in front of him with his fist. Even the judge appeared unnerved by the verdict as he told Morin he was now free to go. After more than one year in jail it seemed that justice had served Guy Paul Morin well. But any joy that Morin and his family may have felt was to be short-lived. The prosecution appealed the decision to the Supreme Court of Canada, basing its argument on inconsistencies in the judge's charge to the jury. Two years later, the Supreme Court ordered that Morin was to stand trial for a second time. Guy Paul would wait three years for that new trial to begin; three years that would reveal just how shoddy the entire investigation into the murder had actually been. Indeed some of the events were almost mystical in nature.

At this point Ruby withdrew from the case, arguing that new trial needed a new perspective. The new defence team consisted of Jack Pinkofsky, Joanne McLean and Elisabeth Widner. The team was surprised to hear that Kenny Jessop, Christine's brother, had found bones at the body site after the initial police search of the area. Pinkofsky wanted the bones tested to insure that they were Jessop's. The only way to prove this would be to exhume the body. This was done on October 30, 1990. The second autopsy proved the bones were Jessop's. The autopsy revealed other shocking evidence. The breastbone had been severed longitudinally, something that could have been done only with a heavy knife. Several vertebra had been sheared through and broken into pieces, a most difficult task to perform. Also multiple cut marks on the neck vertebra had been inflicted from the back. Perhaps the most astounding finding was the massive damage inflicted to the facial bones: this was severe enough to cause unconsciousness or even death. There were also knife marks on several ribs. None of these findings had been reported in the first autopsy. In fact, pathologist John Hillsdon Smith had testified in 1985 that the skull was intact with no fractures.

The implications of these findings were enormous. There would have been massive bleeding at the time of the murder and the killer would have been soaked in blood, as would the area where the murder took place. The killer's crude attempts to dismember the body would have taken at least thirty minutes, a factor that negated the prosecution's argument that Morin had returned from Toronto, committed the murder at the body site and arrived back at his home within the specified timeframe. Adding to the puzzle was the fact that no blood had been found in the soil at the body site. This suggested that Jessop had been murdered elsewhere and the body dumped at the site at some later time. The absence of larvae activity around the body supported this theory. The absence of internal organs was also mystifying. While animals may have devoured them, it was also possible that the killer had removed them for some unknown purpose. All this new evidence would seem to support Guy Paul Morin's claim that he was not Jessop's killer. It also meant that the prosecution would have to rework its evidence against Morin, especially with respect to the timing.

THE SECOND TRIAL

The second trial was preceded by a long and tedious disclosure motion in which the defence attempted to have the case dismissed on the grounds that the police had suppressed evidence favourable to the defence while retaining evidence that could be used against Morin. Considerable evidence was suppressed by the police and prosecution throughout the case. Some important evidence also mysteriously disappeared. The activities of Sergeant Michael Michalowsky, as reported by Makin (1992), are particularly disturbing. Michalowsky, the head of the York Regional Police identification branch, had in his possession two copies of his crime scene notes. The first notebook contained his original notes from the day of the discovery of Christine Jessop's body. The second notebook contained a revised copy of the original notes. This was presumably an attempt to fabricate or suppress various items of evidence. A credit-card receipt had been found at the body site but Michalowsky did not record this in his notes and the receipt was not mentioned by the prosecution at the trial. The defence was never made aware of this receipt, which was later found in Michalowsky's house. A milk carton apparently found at the body site was never mentioned in Michalowsky's first notebook but appears in his second. Michalowsky wrote that the carton was discovered by an officer at the site, but the officer denied this. The defence was not informed of the carton's existence and, for some unexplained reason, it was later destroyed by the police. The underpants found near the body were mentioned in the first notebook but there is no mention of them in the revised notebook. A sample of leaves and debris taken from the bottom of Jessop's shoes was never sent for analysis. Such evidence may have indicated Jessop's whereabouts prior to the murder. The sample was later found in Michalowsky's house. Also found in his home were thirty-five photographs of the body site, which should have been located in the police files. Important measurements taken at the body site by Michalowsky were later proven to be incorrect. In his first notebook Michalowsky indicated that all the missing buttons from Christine's clothes had been found, when in fact only two out of five buttons had been discovered. A small swatch of carpet material found at the body site later disappeared. Michalowsky denied ever having seen the material. Michalowsky also claimed that soil samples taken from the body site had been delivered for analysis on January 11, 1985, when in fact they were not delivered until a year later.

To add to his indiscretions, Michalowsky had not kept the simplest but most important records required of a police investigator in charge of evidence collection: records of trial exhibits and evidence, a record of photos, a list of the items submitted to the Centre of Forensic Sciences, a list of who handled the evidence and a record of taped interviews. Furthermore, neither the York nor Durham police force had a record of the evidence given to Durham by York when the case was transferred to Durham after the discovery of the body.

Other evidence not directly related to Michalowsky was also kept from the defence or lost by the prosecution team. Some small bits of red plastic found on Jessop's clothes and sent for analysis to Stephanie Nyznyk at the Centre for Forensic Sciences simply vanished. Police did not inform the defence about the screams heard at the body site in early October. At the second trial Stephanie Nyznyk testified that a hair found on Jessop's clothes matched those found in Morin's car. When the defence demanded that the hair be turned over to their own forensic expert for analysis, Nyznyk said it had been lost. She had also lost most of the relevant lab sheets for other fibres found on the clothing and in Morin's car as well as 150 slides of hair and fibre samples. The police knew from interviews with young Leslie Chipman that she and Jessop had agreed to meet in the park on the day of her abduction and that Chipman had arrived at the park sometime between 4:00 and 4:30 p.m. but her friend never arrived. Obviously, if Christine had gone to the park early, it is possible that she was abducted from the park and not her home. Chipman's arrival time at the park is therefore important evidence that was never provided to the defence.

The motion to dismiss the case on the grounds of suppressed evidence was heard in London, Ontario, before Judge James Donnelly, an old-school conservative who was well-respected in his community. Perhaps the fact that Donnelly conceded little to the defence during the disclosure motion, while praising the police and the prosecution for the manner in which they conducted the investigation, should have been a warning of things to come. The disclosure motion was lost—Morin would go to his second trial.

The trial began November 5, 1991. The prosecution team, which was led by Leo McGuigan with Susan MacLean assisting, knew that they were as much on trial as Morin. If they were to lose for a second time the case against the man they believed responsible for Jessop's death, there would be a horrendous public outcry over the way the case had been bungled.

Initially, the trial seemed to favour the defence team. Pinofsky's flamboyant style and numbing attention to detail tore to shreds the testimony of the various police witnesses, revealing just how shoddy the police investigation had been. While Pinkofsky may have been scoring points with the jury, he was also trying Donnelly's patience. The defence was also ecstatic when Kenny Jessop electrified the court by disclosing that he and two older boys had engaged in many episodes of sex with Christine when she was between the ages of five and eight. This confession now opened up the possibility that Kenny or his friends had killed Christine because they feared she would reveal their sexual activities. The hair and fibre evidence used against Morin in the first trial was reintroduced by the prosecution, but the defence had their own expert witnesses who argued that this evidence could not link Morin to the crime. With the prosecution's evidence in shreds, the defence and the media alike had every reason to believe Morin would be acquitted. But there was still the testimony of three prosecution witnesses to consider before the trial was turned over to the jury.

Gordon Hobbs, the undercover police officer who had shared a cell with Morin in the Whitby jail, presented evidence that Morin claimed to "Redrum the innocent" (murder spelled backwards). Robert May and Mr. X claimed that Morin had confessed to them. At the first trial Robert May and Mr. X simply appeared to be little more than a couple of con men making deals with the police to help frame Morin. Prosecutor McGuigan knew he had to present May and Mr. X to the court as reformed men who were testifying against Morin because they felt it their civic duty. He had taken pains to tell the two before the trial that there would be no repercussions against them if they refused to testify at the trial. He had the two men state this on the stand in front. The rationale of McGuigan's tactics were obvious. If the jury could be convinced that these men were testifying on their own initiative and not because of some expected reward or favour, then what they said must be true. As the defence was to later learn, it was a marvelous tactic on McGuigan's part. As one of the jurors later stated, "[T]he two inmates went through hell in that trial to give evidence they did not have to give . . . as far as what they gave the jury in evidence I found them to be very credible" (CBC, 1995a).

The defence hoped that by putting Morin on the stand, the jury would see him as a mild-mannered and gentle man who was incapable of slaying a nine-year-old girl. It was a questionable move. Morin appeared nervous and his responses to the questions seemed unemotional and rehearsed. As his testimony progressed, he became more responsive but even when he left the stand for the last time it was impossible to determine his effect on the jury. When all the witnesses had completed their testimonies, the prosecution and defence presented their summations. All that remained was for Donnelly to summarize the case and instruct the jury.

Judge Donnelly had not played a passive role in the trial. He was well-liked with a reputation as a fair and reasonable judge. We will never know for sure if it was a clash of personalities between Donnelly and defence lawyer Pinkofsky that appeared to shift judicial discretion in favour of the prosecution in the Morin case. Yet there is little doubt that Donnelly's demeanour during the trial and his charge to the jury had a tremendous impact on the jury's decision. Courtroom observers detected the warmth Donnelly displayed towards the prosecution team and the repressed hostility he directed at Pinkofsky. When the jury was sitting, it appeared that Donnelly was being impartial in his rulings and, as the trial progressed, the jury came to have great respect for this fair and wise man. This feeling was intensified by the fact that Donnelly was very attentive to the needs of the jury members. However, what the jury never knew was that many of the important decisions made by Donnelly when the jury was absent favoured the prosecution.

An example of judicial bias can be seen in Donnelly's attitude towards Dr. Glenn Cameron, who had diagnosed Robert May as an egocentric liar unable to control his urge to manipulate others. Donnelly's comments left jurors with the impression that the judge regarded Cameron as an incompetent diagnostician. For a jury that had developed a respect for the judge, Donnelly's suggestion that a defence witness was incompetent was probably taken by the jury as truth and may have been a factor in the decision to find Morin guilty.

It was in Donnelly's charge to the jury that the bias inherent in his opinions became obvious. Makin (1992) notes that Donnelly encouraged the jury to endorse the most ludicrous testimony of some Crown witnesses while rejecting important defence evidence. He also instructed the jury to ignore some of the statements made by the defence lawyer, but made no such comments about the prosecution. Perhaps the most damaging statement made by Donnelly against the defence case was his comment that if the jury was vexed by the timing issues raised by the defence they should consider the possibility that Jessop never went home after school: that she was abducted off the street. This possibility had never been introduced by either the prosecution or the defence. With this comment, Donnelly destroyed the very essence of the defence case.

Donnelly also came down on the side of both the prosecution's forensic experts and the Centre for Forensic Science, while negating the testimony of the forensic scientist testifying for the defence. The judge surprised many in the courtroom when he instructed the jury not to take seriously Kenny Jessop's testimony that he and two other boys had been having a sexual relationship with Christine. Furthermore, the judge said little about the vast quantity of evidence lost by the prosecution and the forensic experts.

Donnelly suggested that the jurors consider Mr. X's and Robert May's evidence as truthful because they had testified on their own volition and had nothing to gain by perjuring themselves. He instructed the jury not to give too much credence to the tape of the conversation between Morin and May, which proved that Morin had not confessed to the murder as the prosecution had suggested. The defence was so outraged by Donnelly's charge to the jury that it was to become the basis for its subsequent appeal.

Eight days later, after nine months of evidence, the stony-faced jury returned to the courtroom. The foreman rose and intoned the verdict: "We find the accused guilty of first degree murder." Spectators in the courtroom, including the media, were stunned. Donnelly stared at Morin and intoned the sentence. "Mr. Morin, the law requires that I impose a certain sentence upon you. You are sentenced to life imprisonment without eligibility for parole for twenty-five years" (Makin 1992: 760).

Morin was shipped off to Kingston Penitentiary to begin his sentence while his defence team began the long and arduous process of preparing an appeal. On February 9, 1993, Morin was granted bail, pending an appeal. He was the second person in Canada to be granted bail after being convicted of first degree murder. But the appeal, scheduled to begin January 23, 1995, was never heard. The prosecution had hoped to silence the mounting public criticism of the conviction by submitting the badly deteriorated semen stains found on Christine's underclothes to improved DNA testing. A positive finding would prove once and for all that Morin was the killer. Morin was delighted when he heard of the proposed test. He had asked Clayton Ruby during the first trial if DNA testing could be used to prove his innocence but was informed that the process was still in its infancy and that the stains on the clothing were too badly deteriorated. Now there was some hope. On January 20, two days before the appeal was to begin, the DNA results were made public. The results proved conclusively that Morin was not the person who had raped and murdered Christine. Two days later he was released from prison.

WHY WAS MORIN WRONGFULLY CONVICTED?

Had Guy Paul Morin dated girls, played sports and gotten drunk with the boys on Saturday night he would probably never have become a suspect. But he was different and this difference attracted the police, although they had absolutely no evidence against him at the time. Once targeted and arrested, the police began the process of building a case against Morin. Clayton Ruby, Morin's lawyer at the first trial, made the following comment during a television interview regarding police actions against Morin: "In this case, at the first hint of evidence they just grabbed him and then they started entrapping him and building a case against him . . . . There is no reason to suspect that this kid murdered her as opposed to anybody else in the universe" (CBC 1995a).

The suppression, loss and outright destruction of evidence by the police, prosecution and forensic experts in this case is appalling. Particularly shocking were the actions of Sergeant Michael Michalowsky and the callous handling and loss of evidence by the laboratory technician. The police failure to investigate other suspects is both curious and unforgivable. Jessop's killer will probably never be found at this late date. The deals made with convicted felons Robert May and Mr. X in exchange for fabricated evidence is further evidence of the illegal tactics the police were prepared to use to convict Morin. The police also displayed a lack of professionalism in their initial search of the body site. They overlooked important evidence, such as bone fragments, and they mishandled the body.

We must also consider the obvious lack of skill displayed by those conducting the first autopsy. The results were incorrect and misleading in the extreme. Furthermore, the judicial bias of Judge Donnelly was obvious to many observers and no doubt played a major role in Morin's conviction.

The Morin case, perhaps more than any other in Canadian legal history, represents everything that is wrong with our judicial system. Wrong-doing on the part of police and prosecution, including suppression of evidence, failure to follow leads that would implicate other suspects in the crime, losing evidence, making deals with convicts in exchange for perjured testimony, introducing questionable forensic evidence and experts, and judicial bias all led to the wrongful conviction of Guy Paul Morin.

What most observers of the trial found so incomprehensible about the guilty verdict was that the prosecution had presented only circumstantial evidence along with some very questionable jailhouse confessions from two untrustworthy witnesses. Furthermore, the defence had presented a strong case that certainly should have raised in the minds of the jurors at least a reasonable doubt about Morin's guilt. The questions are obvious. Out of all the people who could have been considered suspects in this case, why was Guy Paul Morin deemed the prime suspect by the police and arrested for first degree murder? Why was this innocent man found guilty after the longest murder trial in Canadian history? The answer lies in the relationship Morin had with the community in which he lived.

Guy Paul Morin's eccentricities caused him to become marginalized from his community. His case is an excellent example of how social intolerance and ignorance cause certain individuals and groups to become the target of negative public attitudes and victims of the forces of social control. Morin was charged and convicted for the murder of Christine Jessop not for what he did, but because of who he was, a person on the fringe, a person who in a time of crisis could be quickly singled out and persecuted. Had Guy Paul Morin behaved like an average young, intelligent, white, middle-class Canadian male he probably would have never become a suspect.

The Morin case illustrates that the judicial system is fundamentally flawed and cannot be fixed with a simple band-aid. Unless there are major changes to our justice system and our value system, there will be more Guy Paul Morins. However, they may not have the good fortune and resources of Morin to overcome the insidious repression experienced by many marginalized people in Canadian society.

NOTE

1. The information for the Morin case came primarily from Makin 1992 and the CBC 1995a television program The Fifth Estate.

6

The Case of
Thomas Sophonow

THE DEFENDANT

A soft-spoken, towering giant of a man, Tom Sophonow can be an
intimidating presence for those who do not know him. He was born
in Vancouver into a working-class family in 1953. The family moved
to British Columbia's Okanagan Valley while Sophonow was quite
young. His father's job as a cook in the lumber camp required him
to be away from home much of the time, so Tom and his sister and
brother were raised primarily by their mother. Although he attended
high school he did not finish grade twelve and, as a youth, spent time
in prison for a number of property crimes. As an adult he abandoned
his criminal activities and wanted to help young boys who could be
headed for trouble. He decided to become a Big Brother but was told
he must first be granted an official pardon, which he applied for and
received. He later apprenticed as a machinist and demonstrated
considerable skill at the job.

Despite the fact that he had turned his life around, Sophonow's
teenage police record may have made him vulnerable to being
targeted by the police for a murder he did not commit. Before being
finally acquitted, he was tried three times and spent four years in
prison. Today Sophonow is again putting his life back in order. He
is happily married with three children and is a supervising machinist
for a Vancouver company.

THE CRIME

It was a few days before Christmas 1981 when twenty-nine-year-old
Thomas Sophonow drove out of Vancouver on his way to Winnipeg
where he hoped to visit his estranged wife and young daughter. A
man who loved children, he was excited at the prospect of seeing his
daughter again. He arrived in Winnipeg about 1:00 a.m. on Decem-

ber 22, little realizing that the series of events about to unfold would ensnare him in one of the most bizarre criminal cases in Canadian history.[1]

At 8:30 on the evening of December 23 the Winnipeg police were called to the Ideal Donut Shop on St. Boniface's Goulet Street. In the women's washroom they found an employee of the shop, sixteen-year-old Barbara Stoppel, lying propped against a wall with a nylon cord tied tightly around her neck. Rushed to a nearby hospital, she was revived but died after spending five days in a coma.

A number of witnesses said they had seen a tall, thin man wearing a mustache and cowboy hat calmly leave the shop sometime between 8:15 and 8:30 that evening. Lorraine Janower, who worked in a drugstore in the mall, had gone to the doughnut shop for her coffee break at her usual time of 8:00 p.m. As she approached she noticed a tall man lock the shop door from the inside and walk to the back of the building. She tried the door, but the man paid no attention to her and proceeded into the washroom. Annoyed, she returned to the drugstore and phoned the doughnut shop, but there was no answer. Suspicious that something was amiss, she watched Ideal Donut from the drugstore window until she saw the same man emerge from the rear of the shop, turn the sign on the door to "closed" and leave. Norman Janower, Lorraine's husband, had also witnessed the man's departure and decided to investigate. He found Barbara Stoppel lying unconscious in the women's washroom.

Several people said they had seen a man in a cowboy hat around the shop about the time of the murder. Myron Zuk told police he noticed a man in a cowboy hat take something from the cash register till before turning the sign on the door to "closed" and leaving the building. Mildred King had come face-to-face with a "cowboy" hurrying through the mall parking lot about the same time as the others had seen him leave the shop. Mr. and Mrs. Paul McDougald claimed that, from their car in the parking lot, they had seen a man wearing a cowboy hat and the waitress walking around the shop at about 8:15. The man then proceeded to the front door and locked it before entering the women's washroom. The waitress followed him into the washroom. A short time later the man emerged, adjusted the sign to "closed," and headed across the parking lot. Others working in the mall told police they had seen a thin, scruffy man wearing a cowboy hat and boots hanging around the mall earlier that afternoon.

From the police perspective the best witness to the events that had unfolded in the Ideal Donut Shop was John Doerkeson. Doerkeson told police he also had tried to enter the locked door of the shop and had noticed the cowboy at the back of the store. However, unlike the others, Doerkeson claimed he was standing at the door when the man came out and told him, "[I]t's O.K. we're just closing for the night" (Malloy 1987: 11). Doerkeson told the police he was very suspicious and followed the man across the parking lot towards a Domo gas station located near the Norwood Bridge. Stopping at the gas station to borrow a baseball bat, Doerkeson pursued the man across the bridge, observing him throw something over the railing to the ice below. The police later discovered on the ice two pairs of gloves and some twine. Somewhere between the gas station and the bridge, Doerkeson decided he could handle the cowboy without the baseball bat and abandoned it before confronting the cowboy on the bridge's narrow walkway. The two men struggled until the stranger drew a knife and threatened to stab Doerkeson, who backed off. Doerkeson claims the man then ran over the bridge. Returning to the Ideal Donut Shop, Doerkeson discovered that Barbara had been killed. At this point he claimed he was so angry that he jumped in a taxi and scoured the streets on the other side of the bridge looking for the cowboy killer. He told police he did not report the incident immediately because he could not locate the man. He said he returned home and drank heavily into the night.

The police were quick to believe John Doerkeson's story about following the cowboy, stopping at the gas station to pick up a baseball bat, struggling with the man on the bridge and seeing the gloves being thrown over the bridge. The gas station attendant confirmed that Doerkeson picked up the bat and returned it some minutes later. However, no baseball bat was ever produced in court, and of all the people who claimed to have seen the cowboy that evening, not one could recall seeing Doerkeson go after the man. Furthermore, none of the dozens of drivers on the bridge that evening reported seeing two men struggling on the bridge. However, something was apparently thrown off the bridge.

Given the number of people who had seen the suspect in and around the doughnut shop at the time of the murder, it would appear that all the police had to do was locate a scruffy-looking man dressed as a cowboy. The police created a composite drawing of the suspect and circulated it across the country, believing that his appearance was so unusual that he would be quickly spotted. Over the next few months however, no cowboy materialized and the public, urged on by the press, began to question why Barbara Stoppel's killer had not been arrested. Angry and frustrated, police continued to comb through their files, looking for that one shred of evidence that would help them identify the killer. Four hundred people were interviewed and approximately one thousand telephone tips were checked out. As well, reward money for information leading to the arrest and capture of the killer had climbed to almost $9,000 (CTV 1986).

Meanwhile, the *Winnipeg Free Press* and the *Winnipeg Sun* kept the issue in the forefront of public consciousness by running periodic updates on the case. Some of these articles contained tongue-in-cheek theories about who the killer might have been. Ross Meder, a writer for the *Winnipeg Sun*, stated that the police were pursuing leads that Stoppel's killer, posing as a *Playboy* Magazine photographer, had asked her to pose for nude photos a few days before her death and that he may have been stalking her the night of the murder. The stories reminded the public that the police were still looking for a suspect. Then, near the end of January 1982, the police got the break for which they had been waiting.

Detective Sergeant Bill Van Der Graff remembered an incident involving a young hitchhiker who had gone missing in July 1981. Thomas Sophonow had contacted the RCMP in Hope, B.C., informing them that he had given a young woman fitting the missing persons description a ride to Winnipeg. The RCMP had passed on this information to the Winnipeg Police, but the girl was never found. Acting on a hunch, Van Der Graff checked his old files and discovered that Sophonow had a police record. Furthermore, the police composite drawing of Stoppel's killer bore some resemblance to the photo of Sophonow in the police files.

Van Der Graff contacted Vancouver police and asked that they informally question Sophonow about his whereabouts at the time of the murder. Sophonow was co-operative, telling the Vancouver police that he had arrived in Winnipeg about 1:00 a.m. on December 22. He had made several unsuccessful attempts by phone to locate his wife and daughter. He visited his wife's parents and left several gifts for his daughter, telling them that he intended to drive to Mexico the next day. The Vancouver police claim that Sophonow also told them that he had stopped for coffee at a doughnut shop in the Goulet Street shopping centre. Sophonow claims he went to a Tim Horton's shop on Portage Avenue. Asked if he knew anything about the Stoppel murder, Sophonow reportedly said he thought the girl's name had been Michelle or Barbara. The police had taken the precaution of warning him that whatever he said could be taken down in writing and used against him. Throughout the questioning they had been jotting things down in their notebooks but what they were recording was not necessarily what he was saying. During the first interview the police took limited notes of the conversation, but did not allow Sophonow to check them for accuracy. The police later explained that they did not let Sophonow check the notes and sign them because they feared he would eat them (CTV 1986). Sophonow was flown to Winnipeg for further questioning, where he was subsequently charged with the Stoppel murder.

THE PRELIMINARY HEARING

At the preliminary hearing Sophonow's lawyer, Rocky Pollock, believed that his client's alibi was so strong the case against him would never be brought to trial. None of the people who claimed to have seen the cowboy on the night of the murder had been able to identify Sophonow in a police line-up. Even John Doerkeson, who claimed to have wrestled with the assailant on the bridge after the murder, failed to identify Sophonow in the line-up. Then, in one of the many bizarre twists in the Sophonow saga, Doerkeson was arrested for failure to pay a traffic fine. It is almost too coincidental that Doerkeson was taken to the same holding cells as Sophonow, where he came face-to-face with the man accused with the Stoppel murder. Only then was Doerkeson able to make a positive identification of Sophonow as the man he struggled with on the bridge. All this took place minutes before Sophonow was to appear in court for his preliminary hearing. Without Doerkeson's positive identification the police had no case against Sophonow and would have been forced to withdraw the charges. Faced with an eyewitness who placed him at the scene of the crime, it was now incumbent upon Sophonow to demonstrate that during his twenty-two-hour stay in Winnipeg he could not have killed Barbara Stoppel.

Sophonow's alibi was that he had arrived in Winnipeg early on the morning of December 23 and later that day had tried to arrange a meeting with his wife and daughter. His stay in the city was to be only a short stopover on the way to Mexico. Failing to meet with his wife and daughter he set out to complete the remainder of his trip. However, a short distance outside Winnipeg his car developed mechanical problems and he turned back. He asked a mechanic at a Canadian Tire outlet on Pembina Highway to check out the problem. While waiting for the car to be repaired, Sophonow walked to a nearby variety store and purchased about forty-five pre-packaged children's Christmas stockings for about a dollar each. He then bought a sandwich and returned to the Canadian Tire. He shared his sandwich with a little girl who was in the Canadian Tire waiting room with her mother. The mechanic then told him that although he had made some temporary repairs to the steering system he did not think the car could make it to Mexico. He did believe the car could make it back to the West Coast if Sophonow drove cautiously. From a pay phone in the Canadian Tire store, Sophonow then made the most important call of his life: a collect call to his mother in Vancouver, telling her he was returning to that city.

Sophonow claimed that he had bought the gifts to distribute to children in the hospitals who would not be home for Christmas. He first went to the nearby Victoria Hospital, but was told by the nurse on duty that they did not have a children's ward. However, she had directed him to the St. Boniface and Misericordia hospitals. After visiting these hospitals, talking to several nurses and leaving the stockings with them for distribution, he had set off for Vancouver. It all sounded like an incredible story being made up by a desperate man. It is interesting that there had been only a superficial attempt by the police to interview the several nurses who saw Sophonow at the hospitals the evening of the murder. Two nurses, Jeanine Gunn of the Misericordia Hospital and Joan Barrett of the Victoria Hospital, said they remember Sophonow delivering the presents that night.

Pollock secured the repair receipts for Sophonow's car and evidence demonstrating that the long-distance call had been made to Sophonow's mother between 7:52 to 7:56 that evening. He had forwarded this information to the Crown prior to the preliminary hearing. However, the prosecution's line at the preliminary hearing was to question why Sophonow had not presented his alibi when questioned in Vancouver and later in Winnipeg at the time of his arrest. The prosecution suggested that Sophonow had created the alibi after his arrest. Sophonow said he felt it was none of their business, adding he had not even told his mother of his plan to deliver Christmas presents. The Crown argued that the simple fact that witnesses had placed him at the scene of the crime was enough to cause him to be held over for trial. Judge Charles Rubin agreed and bound Sophonow over for trial beginning October 18, 1982.

THE FIRST TRIAL

At the trial Crown prosecutor George Dangerfield called various police officers to describe the murder scene and the evidence they had discovered. They related how Doerkeson had reported seeing the man he pursued throw something off the Norwood Bridge and how they had recovered two pairs of gloves and some twine from the ice below. On cross-examination the police stated that they had found no evidence of Sophonow's fingerprints at the scene. Nor did the hair and fluid samples submitted by Sophonow match those found on Stoppel's body.

John Doerkeson's eyewitness testimony against Sophonow appeared much more positive than it had been at the police line-up. He had no hesitation identifying Sophonow as the man he had chased and attempted to drag back to the crime scene.

The prosecution also called on Mr. and Mrs. Janower, Myron Zuk and Mildred King to identify Sophonow as the man they had seen leaving the Ideal Donut Shop on the evening of the murder. Although none of these witnesses had been able to pick Sophonow from a police line-up, they were able to identify him at the trial. As for Sophonow's alibi, Dangerfield admitted that the accused had been at Canadian Tire the evening of the crime and had made a phone call from the premises ending about 8:00 p.m. In a test run, conducted under ideal conditions, the Winnipeg police covered the distance between the Canadian Tire and the Ideal Donut Shop in fourteen minutes, enough time to allow Sophonow to commit the murder. A test conducted by CTV's W–5 program under conditions similar to those on the night of the killing proved that the distance could not be covered in less than nineteen minutes (CTV 1986).

Referring to Sophonow's distributing Christmas stockings at the Victoria, St. Boniface, Misericordia and Grace hospitals, Dangerfield suggested that someone had bought Christmas stockings and someone had taken them to the Misericordia hospital, but it had not been

Tom Sophonow. Dangerfield urged the jury to dismiss Sophonow's alibi as pure invention.

The jury deliberated for twenty-eight hours before informing the judge they had reached an impasse. Judge Louis Deniset had no choice but to declare a mistrial. A date of February 21, 1983 was set for the second trial. Sophonow's application for bail was denied.

THE SECOND TRIAL

For his second trial Sophonow retained Senior Defence Counsel Greg Brodsky. Dangerfield was again Senior Prosecutor. As in the first trial, the first few days of testimony were taken up with police and medical reports, followed by the parade of prosecution witnesses who had seen the cowboy at the Ideal Donut Shop. It is interesting that between the first and the second trial these key witnesses changed their story about the exact time at which they had seen Sophonow at the doughnut shop. At the first trial the witnesses testified that they had seen the cowboy about 8:15 p.m. Unfortunately for the prosecution, this was the time Sophonow was just leaving the Canadian Tire store. At the second trial the witnesses had moved the time of the sighting up to about 8:30, allowing sufficient time for Sophonow to arrive at the doughnut shop. Norm Cuddy, Sophonow's lawyer for his second appeal, stated on the program W–5 that witnesses may have an unconscious tendency to identify with the side for which they testify, and that they may improve their evidence without thinking about it. There is also the possibility that the witnesses were coached to modify their evidence by the police or prosecution.

Brodsky submitted that the photographic line-up that the police presented to the eyewitnesses was prejudiced against Sophonow. Witnesses had been asked by the police to examine a series of ten photographs to determine if they could pick out the cowboy in the Ideal Donut Shop. Brodsky noted that nine of the ten photographs were standard prints; they were of people indoors and had white borders around them and the people depicted were hatless. The tenth photo, the one of Tom Sophonow, was taken outdoors. It was mounted on cardboard, had no white border, was considerably larger than the others and showed Sophonow wearing a cowboy hat.

During this second trial the prosecution called Constable Trevor Black to the stand. Before Sophonow was sent to Winnipeg to be charged, he had been held in a cell by the Vancouver police. Black, acting as a fellow prisoner awaiting deportation to the United States, was placed in the cell in the hope that he could get Sophonow to confess. Black took no notes at the time nor was he wired with any recording equipment. In his testimony he claimed that Sophonow admitted to being in a doughnut shop in Winnipeg and that he had locked the door while he talked to the waitress. This testimony fit perfectly with what the Vancouver police indicated Sophonow had told them during their first interview. Sophonow contended that he was in a different doughnut shop and told the police he had not locked the door of any doughnut shop. The lack of notes or electronic verification of this supposed conversation makes it suspect, as does the fact that Black had not been asked to testify at the first trial.

There was more jailhouse testimony to come. Thomas Cheng, an immigrant from Hong Kong facing numerous fraud and immigration offenses, was put on the stand. He said that he met Sophonow when both men were in the Winnipeg Public Safety Building and that Sophonow confessed to killing Barbara Stoppel. Under cross-examination by Brodsky, Cheng admitted that a couple of days after he submitted his statement to the police he was released from prison and, when he appeared for trial all twenty-eight charges against him, some carrying a maximum penalty of fourteen years, had been dismissed. Within six months Cheng was allowed to voluntarily leave Canada without having to face a deportation order (CBC 1985).

When Brodsky put Sophonow on the stand, he clung to his story about being at Canadian Tire, calling his mother, buying Christmas stockings and distributing them to children in the hospitals. One of the more dramatic moments in the trial occurred when Brodsky approached Sophonow with one of the Crown's exhibits, the gloves found by the police under the Norwood Bridge. When asked if the gloves belonged to him Sophonow declared they did not. Brodsky then asked Sophonow to take the gloves from their package and show the jury whether or not they fit him. It was clear to all in the courtroom that the gloves were several sizes too small for Sophonow's huge hands.

Dangerfield's cross-examination of Sophonow concentrated on his hospital visits. Dangerfield suggested Sophonow's story about the trips to the hospitals was nonsense. Instead he said that Sophonow had gone directly from the Canadian Tire store to the Ideal Donut Shop, where he strangled Barbara Stoppel.

Brodsky countered Dangerfield's accusation by calling Joan Barrett, a ward clerk at the Victoria Hospital. Barrett testified that she recognized Sophonow as the man who approached her at the hospital on the evening of December 23. He had with him two bags filled with Christmas stockings that he wanted to give to the children. She informed him that the Victoria did not have a children's ward but told him how to get to those hospitals that did.

Barrett was clearly a crucial witness for the defence. Her testimony, if correct, would place Sophonow at the hospital at the time of the murder. In fact, her testimony was so important that Justice John Scollin interjected his own question at the conclusion of her testimony, asking her just how sure she was of her facts, considering they had occurred many months before. "I'm dead sure" she said, "I spoke with the man that night" (CBC 1985). Her choice of words would later prove unfortunate for Sophonow.

Scollin's charge to the jury was not favourable to the defence. Scollin did not review Barrett's crucial evidence, but he did make some derogatory comments about her to the jury. He reminded them that Barrett was the only witness in the whole trial that was "dead sure" of her facts, and he said she may not have been so "dead sure" if the authorities had been given the opportunity to check her story. The implication was obvious. The judge was telling the jury that Joan Barrett's testimony should not be taken seriously. Further damage to the defence was incurred when the judge failed to adequately warn the jury that Cheng's evidence was a jailhouse confession and that all charges against him were dropped subsequent to his testimony. It was incumbent upon the judge to inform the jury that Cheng should therefore be considered a suspect witness. In essence, the judge was telling the jury to reject Barrett's testimony but accept that of Cheng. Not surprisingly, the jury returned a verdict of guilty.

Brodsky immediately filed an appeal on the grounds that the judge had overstepped his authority. One year later the Manitoba Court of Appeal ordered a new trial based on the fact that the trial judge did not relate crucial time elements supporting the Crown witnesses' evidence; invited the jury to treat Cheng as an ordinary witness rather than one of unsavoury character; and repeatedly referred to defense witness Barrett as the "dead sure" lady, which denigrated her before the jury. On February 4, 1985, Tom Sophonow was back in court for an unprecedented third trial after spending a year in jail (CBC 1985).

THE THIRD TRIAL

Justice Benjamin Hewak presided over the trial. The prosecution was led by Stuart Whitley and the defence by Brodsky. There was the same parade of eyewitnesses who claimed they could identify Sophonow as the cowboy at the Ideal Donut Shop. In its review of the second trial, the Manitoba Court of Appeal had concluded that John Doerkeson was possibly an unreliable witness. This finding did not influence the prosecution's strategy, as Doerkeson was on the stand once more. Indeed, Doerkeson's memory of the events surrounding the murder seemed to improve with each passing trial. He would now add to his testimony that Sophonow was wearing the poorly-fitting gloves when he entered the doughnut shop. This new bit of testimony meshed with the fact that the police had been unable to find Sophonow's fingerprints at the murder scene.

The prosecution's star witness at the second trial, Thomas Cheng, had departed for Hong Kong after having all criminal charges against him dropped in return for testifying against Sophonow. Undeterred by Cheng's absence, Whitley moved to have his testimony from the second trial read into court as evidence for the third trial. Brodsky argued against having Cheng's testimony read into the record, noting that Cheng was an unreliable witness and had even been charged with additional crimes after the second trial. Judge Hewak ruled in the prosecution's favour, noting that the additional charges should in no way affect the jury's ability to evaluate Cheng's version of Sophonow's jailhouse confession.

Not everything about the third trial was a simple repeat of the previous trials. The prosecution introduced into the third trial new and equally questionable jailhouse confessions. Adrian McQuade testified that in March 1982, while he was in the Winnipeg Remand Centre awaiting trial for possession of stolen goods and break, enter and theft, he met Sophonow. McQuade said that Sophonow confessed to killing Stoppel. Under cross-examination McQuade denied that he was testifying for the Crown in order to have some of the charges against him dropped or reduced. The break, enter and theft charges were subsequently dropped, and he was fined $1,000 for the possession of stolen goods. However, McQuade admitted that he had asked the prosecution for $5,000 in exchange for his testimony. No such payment was made.

Douglas Martin testified that when he and Sophonow were both inmates in the Prince Albert Penitentiary in Saskatchewan, Sophonow confessed his guilt to him. During cross-examination Brodsky forced Martin to admit that he had previously been convicted of perjury in British Columbia. Martin acknowledged that he had a reputation as a liar and a cheater. He also confirmed that he knew Cheng had been granted a stay of proceedings for testifying against Sophonow during the second trial. However, Martin claimed that his only motivation for testifying against Sophonow in this trial was that he felt it was his civic duty to do so.

Other, unsuccessful attempts were made to lead witnesses into testifying against Sophonow. Detective Van Der Graff interviewed Jerry Stolar, a former Winnipeg police officer serving time in Prince Albert Penitentiary for murder. He indicated to Stolar that he had information that Stolar had been friendly with Sophonow while they were both being held in remand in Winnipeg in January 1984. Stolar replied that he did not know Sophonow and had never been in remand with him. Stolar claims that Van Der Graff offered him a deal if he would tell him "what we want to hear . . . you name the deal and we'll work around it." (Malloy 1987: 186). Stolar refused the offer. In a letter to Brodsky dated February 28, 1985, Stolar wrote that another penitentiary inmate had been taken to Winnipeg for interrogation regarding the Sophonow case. Stolar contended that this inmate was first offered a parole and then a pardon if he would testify against Sophonow. He refused and was physically abused by the police.

The extent to which the prosecution was willing to engage in bizarre tactics became obvious when the question of the ill-fitting gloves was again brought to the fore. Crown Prosecutor Whitley argued that since he was about the same build and size as Sophonow and because the glove found below the bridge would fit him, then the glove must also fit Sophonow. The scene represented preposterous logic at its best. It was immaterial whether the glove in question fit Whitley. What mattered was whether the glove fit Sophonow. As if to turn the court into a theatre of the absurd, Hewak overruled Brodsky's objection, asking, "why wouldn't it be of some relevance to know how a glove fits Mr. Whitley's hand compared to how it fits Mr. Sophonow's hand" (CBC 1985). Brodsky noted that the court had not been shown any evidence that Whitley's hand was the same size as Sophonow's. Both the judge and the prosecutor knew that it had been demonstrated at the second trial that the leather glove found under the bridge was much too small to fit Sophonow. But Brodsky's objection was overruled and Whitley's demonstration was allowed to be entered into evidence against Sophonow.

Brodsky wanted to put Sophonow on the stand, but only if the court would approve a highly unusual motion. The intent of the motion was to have Sophonow testify while under the influence of sodium amytal, commonly known as "truth serum." While under the influence of the drug, Sophonow would be examined by a psychiatrist in the presence of the jury. As with any defence witness, the Crown would have the right to cross-examine Sophonow. Although many in the psychiatric profession believe that a person having no desire to deceive will respond truthfully to questions under the influence of this drug, while others believe the reliability of sodium amytal has not been adequately demonstrated. Furthermore, the use of the drug in an open courtroom in Canada would have set a precedent that Judge Hewak was not prepared to consider. The defence motion was denied and Brodsky decided not to call Sophonow to the stand. However, he did have a surprise witness of his own.

Alan Shapiro had been working in the McDonald's restaurant opposite the Ideal Donut Shop on December 23, 1981. Under Brodsky's examination he testified that shortly after 7:00 p.m. that evening he noticed a tall man wearing a cowboy hat, blue jeans and dark-rimmed glasses sitting in a seat that would give him an excellent view of the interior of the doughnut shop. He said he recognized the cowboy as the man who had been sitting in the same seat about a week before. When Brodsky showed Shapiro the composite sketch prepared by the police and asked him how it compared to the man he saw in McDonald's the night of the murder Shapiro said it was "close." Brodsky then asked Shapiro how Sophonow compared to the man he saw in the restaurant. Shapiro replied: "He doesn't" (CBC 1985). Shapiro presented compelling and disturbing testimony. The jury now had to consider that another man fitting the killer's description had been seen watching the doughnut shop while Sophonow was still in Vancouver. Other evidence made available to Brodsky confirmed his belief that someone other than Sophonow had been stalking Barbara Stoppel before the murder.

Fermin Wendles, a Winnipeg taxi driver, told Brodsky that he had driven Barbara Stoppel the short distance between the doughnut shop and her home on several occasions. When he questioned her about taking a cab for such a short distance she told him that it was because of the threatening phone calls she had been receiving from an older man who said he wanted to kill her. Brodsky suggested to Wendles that he relate his story to the Winnipeg police, but when he went to the police station they would not talk with him. Three days later he was picked up and underwent severe interrogation by the police, who demanded to know why he would lie for Sophonow. The experience was sufficiently intimidating and Wendles refused to take the stand.

In summation the prosecution relied heavily on the eyewitness accounts of those who identified Sophonow as the man they had seen leaving the Ideal Donut Shop on the night of the murder. Evidence or testimony that contradicted the prosecution's case was totally ignored in Whitley's summation. The defence, on the other hand, emphasized the fact that Sophonow could not be at the Canadian Tire store and the doughnut shop at the same time. Counsel also pointed out that Sophonow had been seen at the hospital by witnesses at a time that would have precluded him from murdering Stoppel.

After four days of deliberation it was clear that the jury was having difficulty reaching a decision and the possibility of another hung jury was looming. On the fifth day Hewak received a note from the jury indicating that it was unable to reach a decision in the case because one juror, who spoke of having "psychic powers and special gifts," appeared mentally incapable of dealing with the evidence at hand. It appeared that the majority of jury members were asking for Justice Hewak to remove this person from the deliberation process. The prosecution also urged Hewak to remove this person from the jury, if there was sufficient evidence of mental incompetency. Brodsky argued that it was Hewak's responsibility to ensure that the twelve sworn members remain on the jury. When Hewak decided to examine the juror, Brodsky requested permission to cross-examine the jury foreman to determine the motivation behind the note. Hewak overruled this request. Under Hewak's questioning the juror denied saying she was psychic or had special gifts, rather she said that she had a gift for thinking. Hewak concluded that the jury member did harbour thoughts of having special powers and discharged her. The remaining eleven members were then sent back to continue their deliberations, returning a few minutes later with their verdict—guilty.

It had been an unusual trial. Witnesses called by the prosecution had previously been deemed unreliable or questionable by the Court of Appeal. Testimony given at the second trial by a person charged with several crimes, and who had since left the country after having all charges dropped against him, was allowed to be read into the record. The Crown prosecutor was allowed to substitute his hand size for that of the accused without ever proving that they were similar. The judge refused to allow the defense to call Dr. Elizabeth Loftus as an expert witness on the frailties of eyewitness testimony; failed to give the jury adequate warning about convicting an accused on potentially weak eyewitness testimony; and refused to allow the accused to call four witnesses to support his alibi. And, in a final blow to the defence, the judge dismissed the one juror who obviously believed Sophonow was not guilty.

The three chief justices of the Manitoba Court of Appeal, Kerr Twaddle, Joseph O'Sullivan and Charles Huband, all strongly agreed that a number of serious errors had occurred during the trial. Chief Justice Twaddle's decision notes that the trial judge's charge to the jury did not adequately explain the weakness of eyewitness evidence and contained some misdirection. He also wrote that Cheng's bad character and the events subsequent to the testimony made it unjust to have the testimony read to the jury. The decision stated that the judge failed to not only warn the jury of the tenuous nature of the evidence presented by Whitely wearing the glove, but encouraged the jury to consider it. The decision stated that the evidence of three witnesses which would support the accused contention that he was at the hospitals distributing gifts, should not have been rejected. On its own, the Court of Appeal stated, this would have been grounds for setting aside the verdict. It concluded as well that the dismissal of the juror may also have constituted sufficient grounds for setting aside the verdict. The chief justices were emphatic in their opinion that Sophonow was not to face a fourth trial. The Supreme Court of Canada agreed, refusing the Crown's request for leave to appeal.

Thomas Sophonow sat in prison for four years for a murder he did not commit. But, even after the third trial, Winnipeg Police Chief Herb Stephen stated that the police "had brought the proper man before the courts" and that "there should be a fourth trial" (CTV 1986).

WHY WAS SOPHONOW WRONGFULLY CONVICTED?

The senseless murder of sixteen-year-old Barbara Stoppel during the height of the Christmas season raised primordial fears in the hearts of many parents. No child, even an older one, was really safe from predators. As is frequently the case in such circumstances, the police were under considerable public and political pressure to apprehend the killer of this innocent young woman.

Three months after the girl's death, the police targeted Thomas Sophonow. The arrest was made because a Winnipeg police officer had previously dealt with Sophonow and thought he bore a resemblance to the composite sketch created from eyewitness reports of the killer. Interrogated by police, Sophonow's responses plus the fact that he owned a cowboy hat were sufficient grounds for his arrest. This represents the flimsiest of evidence, but from this point on the police would devote all their energies to building a case against him.

There is also the question of the coaching, coercion and intimidation of witnesses by the police. An example is the manner in which witnesses' memories changed over time. At the first trial witnesses claimed to have seen the cowboy leave the scene at 8:00 p.m., a time for which Sophonow could prove he was at the Canadian Tire store. At the second trial the time had been advanced to 8:15 p.m., and at the third trial it was 8:20–8:25 p.m. Expanding the timeframe was essential if Sophonow was to be convicted. We can only speculate as to what role, if any, the police had in widening this window of opportunity, but studies have shown that witness are susceptible to suggestions from the police and others with whom they identify (Loftus 1984).

The method used by the police to get Doerkeson to implicate Sophonow in the murder was also highly irregular and may well have been considered a form of coercion. Doerkeson, who claimed to have struggled with the cowboy on Norwood Bridge, could not identify Sophonow in a police line-up. Only when the police arrested Doerkeson a few days later and arranged to have him brought face-to-face with the man accused of the Stoppel murder could he identify Sophonow as the man on the bridge.

Furthermore, the police photographic line-up could be construed as misleading. The photograph of Sophonow appears to have been presented in a manner that would make it stand out from the other photographs, thus possibly influencing the decision of witnesses viewing them. Also, little attempt seems to have been made by the police to interview witnesses who may have seen Sophonow at the

Canadian Tire store or at any of the hospitals he claimed to have visited. It should also be noted that when the police recorded the time it took to drive from Canadian Tire to the murder scene, they were driving under ideal traffic and weather conditions; conditions that Sophonow would not have experienced on the night of the murder. One may also question why the police never bothered to determine before the trial began if the glove found below the Norwood Bridge fit Sophonow.

The appearance on the stand of Thomas Cheng, Adrian McQuade and Douglas Martin highlights the extent of police intimidation of witnesses in this case. All three of these Crown witnesses had been in serious trouble with the law. It would appear that a deal had been made with Cheng in exchange for his testimony, and McQuade admitted under oath that he had asked to be paid $5,000 for his testimony. How such jailhouse testimony affects the jury is unknown, but without adequate instruction from the judge about the reliability of such evidence one may assume that it played a significant role in the conviction of Thomas Sophonow.

There was also considerable judicial error and bias in this case. The three justices from the Manitoba Court of Appeal ruled Hewak had made serious errors in judgment. Justice Joseph O'Sullivan was of the opinion that the trial judge's discharge of the jury member alone was sufficiently prejudicial against Sophonow's case to negate the conviction. Justice Charles Huband was of the opinion that the trial judge acted prejudicially against the accused by allowing the evidence given by Cheng at the second trial to be read into the third trial. Justice Kerr Twaddle berated the trial judge for inadequately informing the jury about the unreliability of eyewitness identification. Twaddle was also highly critical of the trial judge for allowing the prosecution's demonstration with the glove to be admitted into evidence.

The prosecution must, along with the police and judges, share responsibility for Sophonow's wrongful conviction. Putting Cheng, McQuade and Martin on the stand was the Crown's decision, as was the push to have Cheng's testimony read into the third trial. Furthermore, even a cursory examination of the facts suggests that the prosecution made no sincere attempt to verify Sophonow's alibi about the Canadian Tire store and the hospital visits.

Tom Sophonow was and still is a working-class man. In the weeks following the murder the authorities had been under tremendous public and political pressure to make an arrest in the case. It was Sophonow's criminal record that caused the police to target him as their prime suspect. In many respects Sophonow was marginalized from mainstream society. He had no friends in high places, no money for an expensive defence team and few people who would be concerned about his conviction on skimpy evidence. One may ask whether Sophonow would have been convicted had he been a middle-class man with no criminal record.

After the first trial, Sophonow's original lawyer, Rocky Pollock, recommended that he acquire the services of Greg Brodsky, a highly-skilled and respected Winnipeg criminal lawyer. Brodsky agreed to defend him and to be paid through the Manitoba legal-aid system. Had Brodsky refused the case and Sophonow been unable to obtain his skills, he could still be in prison today. It is a moot point perhaps, but considering the class position and personal characteristics of other wrongfully convicted in this book, the question of class and the quality of defence an accused can afford becomes a key social factor in the determination of guilt or innocence.

The hard evidence in this case makes it quite clear that Sophonow did not and could not have killed Barbara Stoppel. But for those not convinced by the facts presented in court, we can turn to the research conducted for the investigative program W–5. The producers hired Dr. Ben A. Silverberg, director and senior polygraphist for a company called Applied Polygraph Sciences Incorporated, to conduct a "lie detector" test on Sophonow. Silverberg concluded: "My opinion was that Tom Sophonow was telling the truth when he denied any and all criminal involvement related to the strangulation–slaying in 1981 of Barbara Stoppel" (CTV 1986).

Some will argue that the Sophonow case, rather than being an example of justice gone wrong, proves that the system works. The Court of Appeal ruled against the trial judges and Sophonow was released from prison. This interpretation of right and wrong may be appropriate for those who act as society's apologists, but for those who have been wrongfully convicted it is little more than a cover-up. Furthermore, such an explanation buries the more insidious flaws in the social system that led to the wrongful conviction in the first place. To fully understand Sophonow's wrongful conviction a variety of social forces should be examined independently. Thomas

Sophonow was not just prosecuted, he was persecuted. After one preliminary hearing, three trials and four years in jail, even the most detached observer of this case may well conclude that such travesties are not the unfortunate consequence of some simple but correctable errors within our justice system. It is an established fact that the courts prevented the defence from calling expert witness in support of Thomas Sophonow, allowed the jury to hear tainted evidence with no warning or caution and discharged from a properly selected jury of twelve the one person who was not convinced of Sophonow's guilt. The police, the prosecution and the courts used every means possible to convict Sophonow despite strong evidence of his innocence. Like others, Tom Sophonow is the victim of a system that is fundamentally flawed: a system sustained and supported by those we have elected to serve regardless of their political allegiances. There will be those who say that while the system has some weakness it is fundamentally sound, as demonstrated by the fact that Sophonow and some others in this book were eventually exonerated. While there is an element of truth in this argument, in reality it is little more than a simplistic tactic designed to deflect public scrutiny away from a deeper probing into the fundamental defects of Canadian justice.

Even after his acquittal the injustice continued. Sophonow demanded compensation from the Manitoba government as well as an inquiry into his wrongful conviction. The Manitoba government announced new legislation with respect to compensating the wrongfully convicted. Perhaps fearing that an official investigation would result in a huge compensation package for Sophonow, as well as exposing unethical practices within the Manitoba attorney general's department, Attorney General Roland Penner indicated that Sophonow did not qualify for compensation or an inquiry. Penner said that the new regulations required that the individual concerned must prove his or her innocence, and that Sophonow had not met that criteria. Sophonow, he reasoned, although unfairly tried, had not established his innocence. In one stroke, Penner had undercut the philosophical foundation of Canadian justice: the notion that a person is innocent until proven guilty.

NOTE

1. Much of the information for this chapter came from Malloy 1987; CTV 1986; CBC 1985; and personal discussions with Thomas Sophonow.

7

The Case
of Steven Truscott

THE DEFENDANT

There is little reason to suspect that Steven Truscott was in any way an unusual child or that he came from a dysfunctional family. In almost every respect he seems to have been a typical teenager. He had a happy home life, did well in school, was popular with his teachers and had many friends. He had been named his school's best all-around athlete and was to receive a trophy for his athletic accomplishments. His father, a warrant officer in the Canadian military, had been voted the community's man of the year for his work with young people. What made Steven Truscott different from most Canadian teenagers during the 1950s was the lifestyle of his parents. Being a professional military man, Dan Truscott and his family were continually on the move from one place to another, never able to put down roots in one community. Although Steven Truscott was not marginalized from society in the same way others in this book were, he was nonetheless young, vulnerable and available; a child who just happened to be in the wrong place at the wrong time.

THE CRIME

June 9, 1959 offered no relief from the intense heat that had since early May engulfed the Royal Canadian Air Force (RCAF) base about four kilometres southeast of Clinton, Ontario. The heat was bothering twelve-year-old Lynne Harper as she sat down about 5:30 p.m. and quickly downed her evening meal. She had come home with the expectation that her parents would take her swimming at the community pool. When she was told that neither her mother nor father would be able to take her, the girl angrily stormed out of the house. She returned shortly thereafter, but around 6:30 she again left the house in a huff without telling her parents where she was going.[1]

111

Harper knew that Mrs. Nickerson was holding a Junior Girl Guide meeting in the school grounds so she went over to help her. At about 7:00 p.m. fourteen-year-old Steven Truscott, who lived on the base with his parents, rode up near the group on his bicycle and Harper went over to talk to him. Nickerson last saw the two at about 7:10 p.m. that evening. They were walking in a northerly direction and Truscott was pushing his bicycle. The details of what happened after this point have been the subject of debate for over three decades.

The air base was small compared to other military facilities in Canada and was designed as a training facility for communications systems. The base was about two kilometres south of Number 8 highway and was reached by a dirt road leading from this highway. Along this road, about one-half kilometre from the highway, was a bridge that spanned the Bayfield River. The Canadian National Railway tracks crossed the road about 160 metres south of the bridge. Approximately 500 metres south of the tracks the dirt road passed a small bluff of second-growth ash, maple, elm and basswood trees that was known as Lawson's Bush. This bush was separated from the road by a broken-down wire fence. Leading into the northern edge of the bluff from the dirt road was a short lane used by Robert Lawson, the owner of the property, to bring his farm machinery into the nearby grain field. This little lane was known in the community as "the tractor trail."

When Harper failed to return home that evening her father and brother searched for her but she was not officially reported missing until the following morning. Some officers from the Goderich detachment of the Ontario Provincial Police were soon making inquiries. It was left to the base personnel to organize a search party. They combed the area around the community, including Lawson's Bush. Community members were interviewed and the police quickly established that Steven Truscott was the last person to be seen with Harper on Tuesday evening. Truscott was interviewed four separate times that day, and he insisted that he had met Harper in the schoolyard about 7:00 p.m. and that she told him she wanted to see the ponies on a farm a short distance down the highway. He said she asked him to give her a bicycle ride to the highway. He did this, letting her off at the intersection of the highway and the dirt road. He then headed back to town but stopped on the bridge and looked back toward the highway. From there he saw Harper getting into a 1959 gray Chevrolet with yellow license plates. That was the last he saw of her.

On the morning of June 11, a day-and-a-half after she disappeared, Lynne Harper's half-nude body was found in Lawson's Bush, an area that had previously been searched. It appeared that she had been brutally raped and strangled with her own blouse. A search of the area was immediately conducted, although the police did not stake out and take measurements at the body site until a month later. Dr. John Penistan, the district pathologist, briefly examined the body at the site before having it removed for an autopsy. From the contents of the girl's stomach, Dr. Penistan put the time of death at between 7:15 and 7:45 p.m. on June 9, near the time that Truscott was with her. The police investigators, now headed by Inspector Harold Graham from Toronto, suspected Truscott was the killer.

At 6:30 p.m. on June 12, Truscott was picked up and driven to the Goderich, Ontario police station where he was questioned at length. Truscott stuck to his story about giving Harper a ride to the highway and seeing her get into a gray car. Unable to secure a confession from the boy, the police brought him back to the RCAF guardhouse at about at 9:30 p.m. and continued to question him for several hours without either of his parents being present. The law clearly stated that a child facing a serious charge should not be questioned in the absence of a parent or relative. It was during this interrogation that the police decided to have Truscott examined by a doctor.

Dr. J.A. Addison of Clinton and Dr. Brooks, a local practitioner involved in the case from the beginning, examined Truscott and discovered two abrasions, one on each side of his penis, each about the "size of a quarter." Although neither doctor had any previous experience with rape cases, they concluded that the abrasions on Truscott's penis were consistent with rape. Dr. Penistan's estimation of the time of death and Dr. Addison's conclusion that Truscott's injury was caused by rape were sufficient evidence for the police to lay a charge against Truscott. On June 13, four days after Lynne Harper disappeared, Truscott was charged with first-degree murder.

The preliminary hearing against Steven Truscott began on July 13. The Crown's contention that Truscott murdered Harper rested on his admission that he had been with her around the time she was killed and the fact that her body had been found in an area near where they had been seen together on the night of the murder. Truscott's only defence was that he had taken Harper to the highway where she had entered a car and drove east.

Some of those who came forward to voluntarily offer evidence seemed to support Truscott's story. Young Gordon Logan told Crown Prosecutor Hays that on the evening of June 9, he had been swimming at the bend in the river and had seen Truscott and Harper riding towards the highway. Shortly thereafter he had seen Truscott ride back alone. Douglas Oats stated that he had been on the bridge when Truscott and Harper rode by on the way to the highway. Richard Gellatly said he was riding his bicycle when he met Truscott and Harper near the bluff. He said they were heading north toward the bridge. Arnold George said he was down by the riverbank and waved to Truscott and Harper as they crossed the bridge. Allan Oats, Douglas's brother, said he was on his bicycle near the bluff about 7:30 p.m. when he saw Truscott ahead of him on the bridge. All these statements were extremely important to Truscott because they gave him an alibi. It was the Crown's belief that Truscott had not taken Harper to the highway but had turned off the dirt road at the tractor trail and took Harper into the bluff. If this was true, then no one could have seen him with Harper on or near the bridge.

However, testimony was presented that contradicted statements made by Logan, Oats and Gellatly. Fourteen-year-old Paul Desjardine claimed he had seen Truscott alone on his bicycle near the bluff about 6:15 p.m. Two young boys, Kenneth Griger and Robb Harrington, said they had seen and spoken to Truscott between 6:30 and 6:45. They claimed he was sitting alone on his bicycle opposite the tractor trail. Beatrice Griger took a bicycle ride that evening and headed north on the dirt road towards the bridge. She testified that Truscott passed her on his bicycle about 6:10 going towards the bridge. When he reached the bridge he stopped, looked around and then rode back south, passing her again at about 6:30. Obviously, from the Crown's point of view, if Truscott was seen alone on or near the bridge within the timeframe established for Harper's death then he could have killed her in the wood bluff before he rode to the bridge.

The most incriminating statements against Truscott were from his classmate, thirteen-year-old Jocelyne Goddette. She testified that Truscott had made a date with her to go and look for newborn calves in the bush on the evening of the murder but at the appointed time she was unable to go (*R. v. Truscott* 1967: 363). Within this testimony was the inference that Truscott had planned on luring Jocelyne into the bush, but when she was not available he had found a substitute in Lynne Harper.

At the conclusion of the preliminary hearing, fourteen-and-a-half-year-old Steven Truscott was committed to trial in adult court.

THE TRIAL

The prosecution was led by Glen Hays, the defence was in the hands of Frank Donnelly and the presiding judge was Justice R.I. Ferguson. There were strong feelings in Huron County about the murder: the consensus was that Steven Truscott had savagely murdered Lynne Harper. It would have been almost impossible to select jury members who had no knowledge or opinions about the killing. Although it would have served Truscott's interests to have the case tried in a different location, the Truscott family would have been forced to bear all the costs involved in a change of venue. The family could not afford these costs, so the trial took place in Huron County, where most of the potential jurors had some knowledge and opinions of the killing.

The prosecution's case centered on the evidence of Dr. Penistan, Dr. Brooks and Dr. Addison. These witnesses testified as to the contents and the extent of digestion in the victim's stomach. They concluded that the food in Harper's stomach had not been there for more than two hours, which would place the time of death at between 7:00 and 7:45 p.m. Time of death was further substantiated by the state of rigor mortis and the progress of decomposition. The doctors also presented the evidence regarding the injury on Truscott's penis as being consistent with forcible rape.

Dr. Berkeley Brown, an internationally recognized pathologist with expertise in the study of gastro-intestinal diseases, was the star witness for the defence. He disagreed with Dr. Penistan's interpretation of the operation of the human digestive process. It was his contention that it takes the stomach a minimum of three-and-a-half to four hours to empty after a mixed meal. This meant that Harper could have been murdered several hours after Truscott had gone home for the evening.

Jocelyne Goddette testified that she and Truscott had planned on looking for new calves in the bush, but at the last minute she could not go. Truscott's best friend, Arnold George, had initially informed the police that he had seen Truscott and Harper cross the bridge on

June 9, but changed this testimony at the trial. Truscott, he said, had asked him to lie to the police about seeing him and Harper on the bridge. Truscott denied Goddette's and George's testimony, but the jury must have been impressed by the fact that two of his classmates would give such incriminating evidence against him.

Truscott testified that he had seen Harper getting into a gray 1959 Chevrolet with yellow license plates. A police witness claimed that while standing on the bridge Truscott had attempted to identify the makes of various cars on the highway and had failed to do so. He had also been unable to read the license plate number on a test car stopped on the bridge. The fact that Truscott had only claimed to have noted the colour of the plates and not the number seems to have been overlooked several times during the trial (Burtch 1981). Under cross-examination the policeman said that he himself could not identify the make of a car on the highway from the bridge and that the cars he had tried to identify were all traveling at high speed. He also admitted to being unfamiliar with the makes of most cars and to not having had an eye examination in fifteen years.

Gordon Logan, Allan Oats and Douglas Oats all testified for the defence that they had seen Truscott riding his bicycle with Harper on the crossbar in the vicinity of the bridge and that Truscott had returned from the highway alone. Because there was no hard evidence that would have placed Truscott in the bush with Harper, the testimony of Logan and the Oats brothers punched a hole in the Crown's case. The prosecution responded to this challenge by implying to the jury that the testimonies of the three boys were all lies, perhaps fabricated with the assistance of Truscott himself before he was charged with the murder.

After two weeks of hearings, Justice Ferguson gave his instructions to the jury. He offered his opinion that Truscott may have taken Harper to the highway as he claimed, but then brought her back to the bush and killed her. Neither the Crown nor the prosecution had raised this possibility. Ferguson also stressed that because the doctors testifying for the Crown had conducted the autopsy on Harper's body and seen the lesions on Truscott's penis, their testimony must take precedent over that of the forensic experts presented by the defence. Frank Donnelly, Truscott's lawyer, was so incensed by Ferguson's charge to the jury that he accused the judge of telling the jury that, based on the evidence, a verdict of guilty was warranted (Burtch 1981).

Donnelly felt that the prosecution had not made a strong case and was confident that the jury would find his client not guilty. It took the jury only two hours and fifteen minutes to reach a decision. Truscott was found guilty of first degree murder with a recommendation for mercy.

Justice Ferguson was obviously prepared for the verdict and immediately pronounced sentence. Fourteen-year-old Steven Truscott was to be hanged on December 8, 1959. On the last day of November, Truscott received news that his execution had been postponed until February 16, to allow time for an appeal. The appeal was dismissed in mid-January but Truscott was informed a few days later that his death sentence had been commuted to life in prison. Truscott was transferred to the Ontario Training School for Boys at Guelph and remained there until he was eighteen. He was then moved to Kingston Penitentiary to serve out the remainder of his sentence

THE SEARCH FOR TRUTH

Although the Supreme Court of Canada later dismissed Truscott's appeal, many people continue to believe that Truscott did not kill Harper and that the real killer is still at large. In 1966 Isabel LeBourdais wrote the best-selling book *The Trial of Steven Truscott,* in which she presents a compelling argument that Truscott could not have killed Lynne Harper. Her conclusions are based primarily on evidence gathered at the scene of the crime.

Harper's body had been found lying on its back in a slight hollow surrounded by bare earth, grass, twigs and other debris. She was naked except for a blouse and undershirt. Early stages of decomposition were evident and maggots had infested various parts of her body. Her undershirt had been pushed up past her waist and the blouse had been ripped up the left side and shoulder. It had been twisted into a rope and tied around her left jaw in a reef knot. A swatch of material about eight by ten inches square had been cut from the blouse. This piece of cloth has never been found. There was a cut measuring a half-inch deep in her left shoulder and about a tablespoon of still-liquid blood was found on the ground below the injury. Although the undershirt was badly stained with blood, the blouse was not, and there was an almost total lack of blood at the body site except for the minute amount under the shoulder wound and a trace amount on the ground near Harper's pubic area. It is reasonable to assume that Harper had made no attempt to touch the wound on her shoulder because there was no blood on her fingers. This indicates she was probably unconscious or dead when the wound occurred. A long minor scratch extending from above her knee almost to her toes was inflicted after her shoes and socks had been removed.

All the remaining clothes were found at the body site. Her socks had been rolled to the ankle during the process of removal and were lying to the right of the body along with her neatly arranged shoes, shorts and hair band. Whoever removed the shorts had taken the time to pull up the zipper before placing them by the body. The only article of clothing not found near the body were her panties, which were discovered about thirty feet away towards the tractor trail.

Some ash branches had been twisted off the trees and thrown casually over the body, but in no way did these hide it from the view of passersby. Another branch was still hanging partly twisted from the tree, as if the culprit had been unable to break it free. LeBourdais noted that a five-foot-nine-inch man later tried to break the same branch from the tree but could not reach it. Truscott was five-foot-seven at the time of his arrest. The only indication of footprints at the crime scene were those found a few inches below Harper's feet. However, they were not full-blown imprints, but rather representations of pushed-up earth that may have been made by the sole of a shoe if held on its edge. The prosecution suggested at the trial that the impressions were made by Harper's attacker as he lay above her during the attack.

The prosecution was also unable to account for the location of one other personal item of Harper's. Her locket was found hanging from the fence wire that ran along the west side of the bush. The locket clasp was open, suggesting that it was removed from her neck rather than being torn away. There was no evidence that the locket had been snared on the wire as the body was pulled through the fence. The prosecution suggested at the trial that the locket may have been placed on the fence by Truscott to detract investigation away from him.

LeBourdais's central argument is that the only evidence the Crown had against Truscott was that he had given Harper a ride on his bicycle the evening of June 9. Nothing else was ever proven against him. There was, however, evidence that he could not have committed the murder.

Although Harper's undershirt had been soaked with blood from the shoulder wound, there was virtually no blood found at the body site. Also, significant amounts of semen had been found in the girl's body, but none was found on the ground under the body. There was also no evidence that a struggle had taken place at the body site; no clear footprints, no trampled grass or disturbed earth. The only environmental damage was the broken tree limbs that had been laid over the body. All this suggests that Harper had been killed elsewhere and her body brought to the bush after her death. If Truscott was the killer, where did he kill her and how did he transport the body to the bush? He would have had to have carried her because there was no evidence on the body or in the surrounding area that the body had been dragged to its location.

There is also the question of Harper's clothes, most of which had been carefully laid out near the body while the panties had been found some thirty feet away. This raises the possibility that the killer had carried the body to its location and then gone back for the clothes, inadvertently dropping the clothes along the way. Other questions arise. Why had the socks been so carefully rolled down? Surely, this would not be the practice of a frenzied inexperienced rapist. Indeed, why even bother to remove the socks and shoes? Forensic evidence indicated that the missing piece of the blouse had been cut from the garment with scissors, therefore the killer must have had this instrument with him. Remember also that the undershirt was soaked with blood from the shoulder wound, but only minute traces could be found on the blouse. This is a strong suggestion that the blouse had been removed before the shoulder wound had occurred and replaced on the body after death. Again the question is why would the killer take the time to do this and what was the purpose? And what about the absence of blood on Truscott's clothes? Even if the killing had taken place where the body was found, how could Truscott have killed and raped Harper without having at least a trace of her blood on his clothes?

The cause of death also raises questions. There is no question that Harper died of strangulation, but did she actually die as a result of the blouse being tied around her neck? LeBourdais spent many hours and used many blouses, in an attempt to determine how a person could place a sleeveless blouse on the girl's right arm and then pull it into a knot under the left jaw in a manner sufficient to cause death. Every time the experiment was repeated the pressure from the tied blouse was concentrated on the right arm, not on the neck or throat. Her conclusion was that Harper had probably been strangled with another ligature, a belt or a necktie. Most certainly a panic-stricken killer would not methodically place one arm in the blouse and then attempt a difficult strangulation with the remainder of the blouse. LeBourdais proposes that the killer tied the blouse around the jaw in an attempt to confuse the investigation. This attempt to mislead could also account for the body being found in the bush were it would be quickly located. Did the killer know that Harper had been with Truscott that evening and try to direct the investigation towards him by leaving the body in an area that would have been accessible to Truscott?

Truscott's behaviour on the night of the murder must also be considered. After leaving with Harper on his bicycle, he had returned to the schoolyard where he talked to several of his friends. All who talked to him that evening said his behaviour was perfectly normal. After leaving the school he went home at about 8:25 p.m. to babysit his younger siblings. All psychological evaluations on Truscott found him a normal fourteen-year-old in every respect. Is it possible that a normal fourteen-year-old would brutally rape and kill a friend and fifteen minutes later socialize with friends without showing any evidence of stress or excitement? It is a most unlikely scenario.

One must also consider that the ash limbs placed over the body could only have been broken off the trees by a person with considerable strength and who was at least six-feet tall. Such strength would also have been needed to carry the one-hundred-pound girl to the spot in the bush where the body was found. When one considers the above questions the conviction of Steven Truscott is nothing short of alarming.

WHY WAS TRUSCOTT WRONGFULLY CONVICTED?

Once the police had targeted Truscott as the prime suspect there is little evidence that they conducted a comprehensive search for other possible suspects. Truscott's assertion that he had seen Harper enter a 1959 Chevrolet after he let her off at the highway and persistent rumours that Harper had been spotted in Seaforth after she had been with Truscott provoked only a limited response from the police (Trent and Truscott 1979). People living along the highway were questioned and a preliminary search of car makes and license numbers in the Goderich area was carried out by the police. Beyond this, there is little evidence that the police had suspects in mind beyond Truscott (Burtch 1981).

Other evidence of police incompetence can be seen in the police's slowness in organizing a search for Harper after she was reported missing. Furthermore, the lengthy delay in staking out and measuring the body site raises the possibility that vital information and evidence had been lost.

Police testified at the trial that experiments had shown it was impossible to discern either a license plate number or the make of a car from a one-quarter mile distance; the implication being that Truscott was lying when he claimed to have seen the 1959 Chevrolet and the license numbers. The police were aware that Truscott had never claimed to have seen the numbers, only the colour of the plate. As for the make of the car, later independent experiments proved that the distinctive styling of the 1959 Chevrolet could indeed be identified by anyone familiar with the different makes and models of automobiles. To support their testimony that license plates and car makes could not be identified, the police submitted as evidence several out of focus photographs. This misinformation directed at the jury by the police presented Truscott as a liar and probably played a major role in his subsequent conviction.

Highly questionable forensic evidence was presented in this case to determine the time of death. Evidence was also presented by Dr. Brooks that the lesions on Truscott's penis were consistent with sexual assault and that they probably originated sixty to eighty hours before Truscott was examined. The inference of Dr. Brook's testimony was that the lesions were sexual in nature and occurred about the time Truscott was last seen with Harper. The forensic testimony of Penistan and Brooks proved crucial to the Crown's case against Truscott, but their findings have been challenged by other forensic scientists. Dr. Berkeley Brown, a skilled pathologist, testified that Dr. Penistan's estimate of the time of death was far too narrow, noting that there are many variables that can influence the rate of digestion. With regard to the lesions being consistent with rape, it should be noted that neither Dr. Brooks nor Dr. Penistan had any experience with rape-induced injuries. Four medical experts testified at the Supreme Court hearing that lesions are extremely rare in rape cases. Before and after his conviction, Truscott suffered from a skin condition known as dermatitis, a fact that might explain the presence of the lesions (Burtch 1981). A troubling aspect of the forensic evidence is that the doctors conducting the autopsy knew the time of Harper's disappearance before they presented their findings regarding the time of death. They also knew that Truscott was a suspect before his medical examination in the guardhouse. The question as to whether such prior knowledge affected their conclusions remains controversial. In the final analysis, the fact that these doctors were not highly-trained forensic scientists seems to have been overlooked by the court and the jury, which favoured their testimony over that of other forensic experts.

The question of judicial error is also important in this case. Whether Judge Ferguson's biased charge to the jury swayed the decision against Truscott will never be known, but there is some speculation that he overstepped the bounds of judicial propriety (Burtch 1981). The trial of Steven Truscott would seem to highlight the fact that judges are not neutral arbitrators of courtroom combat, but rather opinionated authority figures who exercise their power to sway the decision of a jury instead of upholding the rights of the accused.

In Canada it is recognized that pre-trial publicity can jeopardize the possibility of a fair trial. For this reason, the courts have considerable power to limit such publicity. A recognized legal safeguard for an accused person in Canada is that the effect of pre-trial media attention on the outcome of a trial should be minimized. During the 1995 trial of serial killer Paul Bernardo, the court ordered a change of venue for the trial and imposed a media blackout on certain aspects of the proceedings for the duration. The fact that Truscott was unable to secure a change of venue and was therefore tried in a hostile community was no doubt an important factor leading to the boy's conviction. The RCAF base and the nearby town of Clinton were typical of rural Ontario during the fifties decade. Homicide was a rare event in this part of the province, so the brutal sex slaying of a twelve-year-old girl sent a wave of horror and panic through the population. The depth of the panic can be seen in the fact that on the same day the body was discovered, the Ontario attorney general offered a $10,000 reward for the killer "dead or alive." This was the largest reward ever offered by the province for information leading to an arrest and conviction. Truscott's quick arrest allayed the immediate panic, but it also soothed the community conscience.

Many people were therefore quick to conclude that Truscott was guilty even before he was tried. One might well ask if Truscott would have been convicted if he were the son of a prominent family backed by wealth, prestige and connections with the politically powerful. A child from a privileged family would have been defended by the legal counsel capable of intimidating those who wanted to twist and fabricate the evidence to build a case against him. Had the police and others involved in the early stages of this case treated a child of wealth as they treated Truscott, they may well have been charged under the law.

To this day the murder of Lynne Harper and the trial of Steven Truscott can generate heated debate among those interested in Canadian crime and justice. In the minds of many, Truscott was as much a victim in this tragedy as Lynne Harper. Sadder still is the fact that Harper's killer may never be brought to justice. As for Truscott, after ten years in prison he was released on probation, changed his identity, got a good job, married and now has a family of his own. But the cloud of his conviction still hangs over him.

NOTE

1. Isabel LeBourdais's 1966 best-selling book *The Trial of Steven Truscott* and Bill Trent and Steven Truscott's *Who Killed Lynne Harper* (1979) were the basis for most of the information contained in this chapter.

8

Conclusion

Wrongful convictions can be understood on two levels of analysis. The first level involves the professional and bureaucratic wrong-doing within the justice system, which includes the targeting practices of the police, the suppression of evidence, coercion and intimidation of witnesses, falsified forensic evidence, judicial malpractice jury tampering, and prosecution and defence misconduct. The second and more important level analyzes the way Canada's persistent systemic social inequality causes certain individuals and groups to become socially, politically and economically powerless. These marginalized people become the most frequent victims of wrongful conviction.

A GROWING AWARENESS

In recent years extensive media coverage and several best-selling books have resulted in a growing public intolerance for wrongful conviction. Books on the Donald Marshall, David Milgaard and Guy Paul Morin cases by Michael Harris (1986), Carl Karp and Cecil Rosner (1991) and Kirk Makin (1992) respectively focused public attention on these miscarriages of justice. Earlier publications dealing with the wrongful conviction of Wilbert Coffin (Hebert 1964) and Steven Truscott (LeBourdais 1966) were critical indictments of the Canadian justice system, but they did not raise public consciousness to the same level. That the recent works have been popular with the public may be a sign that people are more prepared to be critical of our justice system.

Another source of the growing public awareness is the extensive coverage of recent wrongful convictions by both the CBC and CTV television networks. Since the late 1980s several investigative reports on the subject by CBC's *The Fifth Estate* and CTV's *W–5* have raised public sensitivity to the issue and eroded much of the apathy and ignorance surrounding wrongful convictions.

The fact that both the state and the legal profession have recently been shamed into taking action against some judges and lawyers has also heightened public awareness about a variety of problems endemic to our justice system. Judges, for example, are now being taken to task by their own peers for professional misconduct. Recently, one judge was reprimanded for racist and sexist comments made during a trial, while another was chastised for unacceptable behaviour directed at female lawyers and court workers. Such activities and attitudes on the part of a judge would once have gone unreported. Judges were, and still are, at the top of the social ladder, and it would have been unseemly for the media to question their behaviour. Although lawyers were never accorded the same esteem as judges, their rank nonetheless demanded respect. Until recently, their misconduct was seldom challenged by the public or the media. Fortunately, judges, lawyers and other professionals no longer enjoy the protection of media silence. The public now demands that they be held responsible or their wrong-doing.

Unfortunately, it is too early to suggest that this emerging public awareness will develop into a full-blown movement dedicated to the elimination of wrongful convictions. Taken together, however, these signs suggest that the public is now aware that wrongful convictions are more frequent than one was once generally believed. That being the case, the question becomes obvious. What can be done? What are the implications for change that will prevent future wrongful convictions? The answers, however, are less obvious.

WHAT CAN BE DONE:
PUNISHMENT, LEGAL CHANGE, SOCIAL TRANSFORMATION

PUNISHMENT

While honest mistakes have and will continue to result in wrongful convictions, the evidence presented in the preceding cases suggests that much of the wrong-doing is rational and deliberate. Wrongful convictions appear to thrive in those situations where "doing the right thing" becomes secondary to gaining a conviction and earning a promotion. A professional has a strong motivation to deviate from the legal norm if the risk of detection for misconduct is low and the rewards are high. If the risk of detection is high and the potential rewards low, incentive for professional misconduct should also be low. It is necessary that detection and punishment of such acts be vigorously pursued by the state. To date, the system has been unwilling to adequately punish those guilty of professional wrong-doing. Police Chief John MacIntyre and Sergeant Michael Michalowsky were allowed to slip out of the system and avoid punishment. Indifference to internal corruption and bureaucratic malfeasance appears to thrive in those jurisdictions that lack the sophistication and will to weed out the wrong-doers.

If we are to limit wrongful convictions to honest mistakes, then we must ensure that the laws that prevent the suppression and altering of evidence, witness intimidation, jury tampering and other judicial wrong-doings are better enforced. The state must demonstrate to would-be wrong-doers and the public alike that it is prepared to maintain the integrity of the justice system by implementing stronger means of detecting wrongful convictions. Police, prosecutors, lawyers and forensic experts who intimidate witnesses; fabricate, conceal or distort evidence; or otherwise subvert the process of justice and break the public trust should not escape criminal and civil sanctions. The CBS television program *60 Minutes* aired a report in October 1997 about the wrongful conviction of Rolando Cruz. He was found to be wrongfully convicted when a high-ranking police official who worked on the case admitted that the police and prosecution lied about evidence that had convicted Cruz. He had spent ten years on death row. In 1997 a grand jury indicted three prosecutors and four police officers involved in the case for perjury and obstructing justice. They are now awaiting trial (CBS 1997). The state should undertake a comprehensive review of all cases handled by officials who have been found guilty of actions leading to a wrongful conviction. Such action has recently been taken against the Ontario Centre for Forensic Sciences after it was discovered that a centre technician suppressed evidence that would have damaged the Crown's against Guy Paul Morin. The provincial bar associations should initiate similar reviews of past cases handled by lawyers found to be involved in wrongful convictions. Disbarment for these individuals should be a possible penalty.

Those at the highest level of the justice system must be made to know that they cannot hide behind the authority of their position by relegating the moral and ethical responsibilities to those below, and then claim ignorance about what others under their authority were doing. Ministers of the Crown and senior civil servants should be held accountable for the misdeeds of their subordinates because they set and control the conditions under which the subordinates commit the malfeasance. The police, most lawyers, forensic scientists and others involved in the justice system are usually evaluated by their superiors on the basis of the number of cases they have helped solve or win. The more cases won the higher the economic and social rewards, including the esteem of one's peers. Likewise, civil servants are evaluated and promoted on the basis of a "job well-done." What is called for is a reconsideration of what constitutes a job well-done. The number of cases solved or won will likely remain an important consideration in evaluating police and lawyers, but seeing justice done must somehow be made a priority over cases won. It is the responsibility of the ministers of the Crown and senior civil servants to set the ethical standards for their subordinates and to ensure that these standards become the basis for peer recognition and career advancement. We can expect the number of wrongful convictions due to professional and bureaucratic misconduct to drop dramatically only when those in charge are denied the use of scapegoats to hide their malfeasance; when accountability, mutual trust and professional pride are rewarded; when professional violations are reported without fear of reprisal; and when penalties are swift and just.

Outside the professional system, eyewitnesses and others who are found to have wilfully fabricated or distorted facts should be prosecuted for perjury. The key word here is "wilfully." Witnesses who have been coerced by police or other officials into perjuring themselves are themselves victims of the system and should not be expected to suffer further by being charged with perjury.

MAKING LEGAL CHANGES

Legal-aid services have become commonplace throughout Canada in recent years. The concept has its roots in seventeenth-century England and is based on the democratic concept of equal justice for all. Indigent defendants, unable to retain legal counsel, would have one provided by the state (Snider 1985). In Canada, several models for delivering legal services to the indigent have emerged. New Brunswick and Alberta have adopted the pure "judicare" model, which provides for private lawyers to act on behalf of the indigent and to have their fees and expenses reimbursed by the provincial government. The "clinic" system retains staff lawyers and paralegals to provide legal services for indigents. Nova Scotia, Prince Edward Island and Saskatchewan use the clinic system. Ontario, British Columbia and Manitoba are basically judicare systems but do have a limited number of staff lawyers. Newfoundland and Quebec operate fundamentally clinic-based systems with a judicare component.

Unfortunately, none of the above models has succeeded in achieving legal equality for the marginalized peoples of our society. Laureen Snider (1985) argues that social reforms such as legal aid are doomed to failure because they have as their constituency the isolated and marginalized welfare mothers, the unemployed and the visible minorities, all of whom are politically, socially and ideologically weak. Snider further notes that the failure of other reforms, such as the prisoners' rights movement, diversion and search warrant reform, can be explained in the same fashion—they are aimed at powerless populations.

This is not to suggest that some limited benefits have not materialized through the development of legal-aid programs. Many marginalized people have been kept out of prison with the assistance of legal-aid lawyers, unpaid wages have been recovered, divorces have been secured and so on. Also the presence of legal-aid lawyers in court may have curbed some of the worst abuses experienced by the poor who go through the system. But the essential point remains: there has been little real structural change in the legal system as a result of legal aid (Snider 1985).

The question is not simply whether all classes have equal access to legal representation, but rather, how equal is the representation? We have seen evidence that those represented by legal aid are unlikely to receive the same quality of defence as those who can afford the best private lawyers (Reiman 1990; Huff et al. 1996). Legal equality demands that all people have access to the same quality of counsel as far as is possible, but this has not been achieved under legal aid. Legal-aid lawyers working out of clinics have too many cases and too little time. This creates a situation in which the client is frequently encouraged to plead guilty (Cunningham and Griffiths 1997). Legal aid, in the final analysis, has perhaps served the needs of the state and the middle class more than the needs of the marginalized. Legal-aid services create jobs for lawyers, paralegals and secretaries while the state is perceived as being concerned about the plight of the poor by providing them with legal services.

Given the rather dismal record of legal aid, are there any reforms that might better insure legal equality for all? The problem is complex and there are no band-aid solutions. What is needed is a more radical approach to legal reform, one that is characteristic of the health care reforms of the 1960s in Canada. All lawyers, like doctors, would work under a fee-for-service system paid for by the state. Clients, regardless of their ability to pay, would have the right to retain the lawyer of their choice. There is little doubt that the legal profession would oppose such reform, and would invoke the same arguments against universal legal care that the medical profession used when they fought against medical reform. But even this radical approach, if implemented, could have its problems. Universal legal care paid for by the state raises the spectre of the state being in the position of paying for both the prosecution and defence in all civil and criminal cases. Even a powerful and neutral watchdog agency may find it impossible to oversee and manage such a cumbersome bureaucracy.

The poor are also at a distinct disadvantage when it comes to gaining access to forensic science expertise. The prosecution, backed by the formidable power of the state, has access to the best forensic techniques available. Likewise, the wealthy and powerful also have the ability to pay for the latest scientific technology to prove their innocence. The poor, however, are unable to afford the luxury of such costly procedures. Should not the concept of equal justice for all include not only equal access to legal representation but also equal access to technology? We argue that it should, and that it be provided through the same mechanism as universal legal care.

There has been some action by the state in recent years in response to several exposed wrongful convictions. The negative publicity generated by the Donald Marshall Jr. case, and more recently the Morin case, forced the governments of Nova Scotia and Ontario to hold public inquiries. At the time of writing the Morin inquiry is still in progress but the recommendations of the Royal Commission on the Donald Marshall Junior Prosecution (Royal Commission 1990) are informative. However, some scholars claim the Marshall inquiry fell far short of its potential for bringing about change to the justice system (Mannette 1994; Henderson 1992; Wall 1992). Joy Mannette (1994) suggests that the report may even be counterproductive to the process of justice:

> [T]he role of official discourse is to assign blame in terms of the temporary failure of an essentially reformable system. Emphasis on human fallibility is often made to reinforce the notion that had actors adequately discharged their function, the crisis which has led to state intervention would have been averted. Having been seen to publicly and authoritatively take charge of the assignment of blame, the state process of official disclosure transforms an ideological phenomenon (i.e. eroded public confidence in judicial process) into a material event (i.e. the inquiry and its report). The material event is worked up according to principles of administrative rationality and legal coherence (e.g. the use of lawyers, judge, quasi-judicial format, etc.). (420)

Bob Wall (1992) suggests that even when forced to look at the issue of racism, the commission's report played down the endemic problems plaguing the justice system:

> [The Liberal-progressive ideology prevalent in Canada today] holds that the system is neutral or value free. Justice is the blind woman holding the scales. If something goes wrong, then the proper response is to tinker with that part of the system which has broken down. By focusing attention on individual offenders, criticism of the broader aspects of the social structure surrounding the issue is deflected. So, in this case, a mandate focusing on the specific problem of Marshall could be seen as averting attention from a general malaise in the justice system. (22)

Indeed, an independent review board such as that recommended by the commission is essentially reactive, not proactive. The board would attempt to redress wrongful convictions after the fact rather than seek to isolate and correct the initial source of the problem. It would be treating the symptoms but ignoring the disease. As presented, the commission's recommendations depict Canadian justice as being an essentially sound institution that sometimes malfunctions, thus negating the possibility of any fundamental change within the system itself.

Regardless of the above criticism of the report of the Royal Commission on the Donald Marshall Junior Prosecution (Royal Commission 1990), the commission's existence must nonetheless be considered a step in the right direction. By initiating an official inquiry into Marshall's prosecution the state has officially recognized that the criminal justice system is flawed and that racism and bigotry were major factors in Marshall's wrongful conviction. Several of the report's eighty-eight recommendations attempt to deal with the issue of racial inequality in the justice system. In the document *Response to the Recommendations of the Royal Commission on the Donald Marshall Junior Prosecution* (Government of Nova Scotia 1990), we see that a number of the commission's recommendations have either been implemented or are being considered by the Nova Scotia government.

The commission recommended the adoption of a policy on race relations within the departments of the attorney general and the solicitor general, which would eliminate inequalities based on race. The government of Nova Scotia accepted this recommendation and has adopted a policy on race relations aimed at employment equity and a more harmonious relationship between the justice system and all Nova Scotia communities (Government of Nova Scotia Response to the Recommendations of the Royal Commission on the Donald Marshall Jr. Prosecution 1990: 5).

The commission recommended the establishment of a Cabinet committee on race relations and the government agreed with the recommendation (6). It also agreed with the recommendation that the Dalhousie Law School minority admissions program receive additional funding and that there be increased appointment of visible minority judges; professional education for Crown prosecutors, explaining systemic racism and reducing such discrimination in the justice system; enhanced police training regarding visible minority issues; and the implementation of an Alternative Penalty Act, which would address the particular needs of Aboriginal and Black offenders (6–9).

The Nova Scotia government also agreed with the commission that more Aboriginal people need to be hired in correctional services and that existing correctional workers be given sensitivity training regarding the needs of minority peoples. There was a recognition of the need for funding for an Aboriginal court workers program and for a regular sitting of provincial courts on reserves. It was also agreed that the advice of a Native justice committee should be sought by judges sentencing Natives (10–17). The recommendation of the commission that the government establish a Native constable program was already in the developmental stage by the RCMP at the time of the commission report.

The wrongful conviction cases presented in this book emphasize that improper police interrogation, incompetent police handling of evidence at the murder scene and afterwards, improper disclosure and improper judicial charges are key factors leading to wrongful convictions. The Royal Commission (1990) report does respond to these concerns, although sometimes in a muted fashion.

Regarding improper police interrogation techniques, the commission recommended that interrogation sessions be videotaped and that it become standard practice for police supervisors to review with the investigating officers the progress of the investigation (48). These suggestions have now been incorporated or are being considered by a number of police departments. The commission also recognized the incompetence of the police in handling evidence and has recommended fuller training for police officers and the development of a standardized code of ethics for all police services (50). Whether the police training facilities have actually followed up on this recommendation is almost impossible to measure and police spokespeople (informal telephone interview RCMP training department) claim that they have always had a code of ethics. Basically, the commission's recommendations centred on police–minority relations rather than improving the fundamentals of policing techniques and evidence handling. Regarding improper disclosure by the Crown, the commission recommended four major changes to the Criminal Code of Canada (Government of Nova Scotia Response to the Recommendations of the Royal Commission on the Donald Marshall Jr. Prosecution 1990:29–30). When questioned about the implementation of these recommendations, the solicitor general's office in Ottawa (telephone interview with solicitor general's office) stated all of the recommendations were being considered but were vague about actual implementation. However, it was stated that the accused will soon have the right to receive a copy of any statement made by a person whom the prosecutor intends to call as a witness and to receive any material or information known to the Crown that negates the defendant's guilt. In terms of improper charges to a jury by a presiding judge, the commission limited its recommendations to the abolition of summaries given by trial judges and the abolition of the practice of providing trial judges with copies of the preliminary inquiry transcripts.

It is not the purpose of this book to review all the findings and recommendations of the commission. However, it is worth noting that the Nova Scotia government agreed with almost all of the eighty-eight recommendations in its 1990 response to the commission Report (see Nova Scotia Government 1990). How many of the recommendations have resulted in real changes to the justice system is difficult to determine. For example, the government did increase funding to Dalhousie Law School for its minority admission program, but the immediate effect of this measure on race relations or benefits to minorities within the justice system are almost impossible to measure. Furthermore, many of the recommended programs, such as educating Crown prosecutors about systemic racism, do not lend themselves to forced compliance and are voluntary on the part of the Crown prosecutors. How many attend such programs and how effective they are in combating systemic racism is also difficult to determine.

While primarily an attempt at political damage control, establishment of the Royal Commission on the Donald Marshall Junior Prosecution was nonetheless an admission by the state that the justice system does not treat all Canadians equally. In this sense the commission's report (Royal Commission 1990) represents an important social document, which may be viewed as a catalyst for a number of policy initiatives on Aboriginal rights.

Another necessary legal change is the mandatory compensation of individuals proven to be wrongfully convicted. While Donald Marshall Jr. received limited compensation from the state for his wrongful conviction, the Sophonow and Milgaard cases clearly demonstrate that the state is quite prepared to dodge this responsibility by claiming that "not proven guilty" is distinct from "innocent." The state must be legally prohibited from hiding behind such legal technicalities and meet its moral responsibility to compensate handsomely and quickly those who have been victimized. Such compensation must be based on lost wages, incurred legal expenses, damage to one's reputation and honour, separation from family and community, and the mental and physical torment of incarceration. It should also be tax-free.

But we must be on our guard. The state is not a social reformer and cannot be expected to be in the vanguard of social change. Nor should social reformers hope to be able to utilize the state to mobilize marginalized peoples into a struggle to ameliorate their position. What frequently gets neglected in people's efforts to reform the system is the problem of reform itself.

The struggle for human equality challenges existing power relations within the social structure. It will be most strenuously resisted by those groups in whose interest the law works best. Paradoxically, by transferring the resolution of wrongful convictions to legal channels, social activists shift political action away from the struggle for equality and towards the legal machinery of the state. They are frequently overcome by this process. The moral struggle for equality must not be subjugated by the class-based legal restrictions of legal discourse.

There is always the danger of the state usurping potentially powerful social movements. In the process, the reformers are transformed into middle-class administrators overseeing some new social program. All too frequently we see a "social problem" moving into the public domain where it becomes institutionalized and the movement itself extinguished. Jan Barnsley (1994) believes this state appropriation has occurred with some segments of the women's movement. Similar American state intervention in the Mobilization for Youth Project and the War on Poverty, both potentially strong movements for social change, occurred in the 1960s. The Company of Young Canadians had a similar history. The lesson of these past failings is that governments are incompetent agents of social change. The political struggle for social equality must be maintained and controlled at the grassroots level. It should not be leased to a state-administered bureaucracy that is out of touch with the people initiating the movement. Progressive social change comes from the will and actions of the people. Activists must not be lulled into believing the struggle has been won simply because some progressive concepts have been codified. The law, like fire, can be friend or foe, and requires continued vigilance.

But state usurpation of a social movement is not a foregone conclusion. The leaders of the Canadian Aboriginal movement seem aware of the above pitfalls and are refusing to let the state direct the course of their struggle. With their continuing efforts towards self-determination they have become a powerful social movement, seeking recognition as self-governing nations with economic control over all lands they claim. Any diminution in this movement for self-determination would surely be tantamount to the Aboriginal peoples acquiescing to cultural genocide.

TRANSFORMING SOCIAL INEQUALITY

There is ample evidence that Canada is a class-based society and that the inequality between rich and poor, privileged and non-privileged is widening (Knuttila 1996; Hunter 1981). Figures from Statistics Canada show that the lowest 20 percent of the population receives only 5 percent of all income, while the richest 20 percent receive about 44 percent. In addition to economic inequality, there are also inequalities of prestige, privilege, power and race. There is a certain prestige or honour associated with an occupation that places an individual within a particular social stratum. Most people would agree that there is more prestige attached to being a lawyer, doctor or airline pilot than to being a carpenter or plumber. Doctors, lawyers and airline pilots are therefore in a higher social stratum than the plumber. Along with inequalities in income and prestige, social scientists also note an unequal distribution of power in society. Power in this sense means the ability of an individual or group of individuals to exercise their will over others, even in the face of resistance. The unequal distribution of income, prestige and power, as well as systemic racism within Canadian society, are the bases of structured inequality and marginalization.

But social inequality in all of its manifestations is not necessarily a static condition. It can fluctuate with changing economic conditions and shifting political ideologies. In the early 1970s in the United States, Canada, Britain and Australia there began a political and ideological shift to the right that has been legitimized as the new establishment ideology. (Havemann 1986) This movement, which proclaimed the demise of New Deal liberalism, promoted a moral outrage about crime and advocated a tough law-and-order approach to social reform. In particular, it called for tougher controls on crimes of the lower class; harsher methods of punishment, including increased use of, or return to capital punishment; and a general expansion of state measures of control.

In Canada this ideological perspective is best represented by the politics of the western-based Reform Party and its anti-gay, anti-welfare, anti-Quebec, anti-abortion and pro-capital punishment agenda. The growing popularity of the right-wing party is due primarily to the concerns of the middle class and the new working poor, who have experienced a continuous erosion of their income and lifestyle under the "restructuring" programs of government and industry. Seeking an explanation and a solution to their plight, many working poor buy into the right-wing argument that their problems are rooted in the state's coddling of the unemployed, welfare mothers, First Nations people on the reserves, young people and criminals. Evoking such racist and sexist class-based imagery promotes a generalized ideology about crime and criminals that mystifies the true causes of crime, downplays corporate crime and focuses on the crimes of the lowest class.

However, despite the New Right proclamation that cuts in social spending, privatization of some social services and targeting of expenditures on marginalized groups have brought an end to the welfare state, the agenda has not been successful. The right's law-and-order policies have not lowered the crime problem as promised. In the case of property crime, the rate has actually increased. Potentially, there could be some discontent with the law-and-order approach to crime control.

What then can be done in both the short and long term to defeat the right-wing law-and-order agenda and create a more equitable system of justice? It is our belief that changes to the criminal justice system, which would make it more fair, cannot be considered in isolation from the fundamental social changes required to make society more equitable. The goal of social equity is difficult and many obstacles will be faced, but it is our belief that the process must begin with small groups acting collectively for a cause. Such groups have historically been the nucleus of meaningful social movements. For example, the women's movement began with small collectives of women, which later merged to form stronger groups to effect changes in the law and thus enhance the social position of women in Canada.

Likewise, the struggle of First Nations peoples began with small groups, and today has successfully forced legal changes in the direction of Aboriginal self-government. The goal of these groups must be the elimination of, or at least the drastic lowering of, social inequality in Canada. Only when we have equality of opportunity will wrongful conviction and other evils of the justice system be suppressed.

But will this be done? How are these groups to be formed and of whom will they consist? Changes to the system that will ensure a higher level of social equality must come from the people who will most benefit from the change. Unfortunately, it is here that we also find a key obstacle to a viable social movement to eliminate inequality. The needs of the poor and marginalized are not a high priority for governments and most of the middle class. Furthermore, marginalized peoples, by definition, are not organized to fight collectively for their rights, and their poverty and lower levels of education make it difficult for a few well-meaning middle-class reformers to assist them with organizing. It is naive to say that inequality will be eliminated by raising the consciousness of the marginalized through education and making them aware of the source of their problems. This is not to suggest that education would not be a factor in the solution; it would, but how to educate the marginalized and raise their consciousness to the level of collective action has yet to be determined.

Snider (1985) argues that reforms fall into two major types, "positive" and "negative," and that much of the failure of past reform movements is a result of placing too much emphasis on the "positive." For judicial reform, the "positive" measures would include a call for more training schools, more prison psychiatrists, more drug treatment programs and so on. Snider (1985) suggests these reforms do little to revamp the system and may even add to the oppression of the underclass by increasing the power of the institutions of social control. Reformers, whether small groups or large, must resist the temptation for "positive" reforms because such institutions work in the interests not of the marginalized but of the state and the middle class who are employed by these institutions (Snider 1985). "Negative" reforms, on the other hand, are aimed at abolishing those conditions within the system that assist in the repression of the marginalized. Examples of "negative" social reform include working for shorter prison sentences, abolishing censorship and using legal aid to secure rights rather than privileges because "privileges invariably become one more tool with which to control ones clientele" (Snider 1985: 231).

Perhaps the strongest force for fundamental changes overcoming class and race inequalities will come from a union of academics, media and citizen groups concentrating on "negative" reforms. Some university curricula, such as the one at Cardozo Law School in New York, have been changed to include a course on wrongful convictions. The Cardozo class was started by Barry Scheck, the DNA expert for the O.J. Simpson defence team. In Canada, York University's Osgoode Hall Law School has implemented the Innocence Project, a two-semester, nine-credit-hour clinical program in which students take on cases to determine if a wrongful conviction has occurred. Incorporated into the course is an analysis of the forces that may lead to wrongful convictions. Professor Dianne Martin, co-director of the program, states that the program is a unique pedagogical and political experience for law students. An increasing number of academics are researching and publishing works on the need to reform the social structure. The media has been sensitized to the fact that reports focusing on such social issues are popular with the public. Academics knowledgeable on the topic of social inequality are frequently called on by the media, as are representatives from such community groups as the Saskatchewan Coalition Against Racism (SCAR). Such a union of forces may eventually lead to the public understanding that the present law-and-order campaign espoused by many politicians and some religious groups represents a carefully orchestrated shift to the ideological right. This right-wing shift directs people's fears and concerns about crime and personal safety towards those living on society's fringes.

References

Anderson, Patrick R.L. and Thomas Winfree Jr. 1987. "Criminal Justice Scholars as Expert Witnesses: A Descriptive Analysis." In Patrick R.L. Anderson and Thomas Winfree Jr. (eds.), *Expert Witness: Criminologists in the Courtroom*. Albany, NY: University of New York Press.

Ares, C.E., A.A. Rankin, and J.H. Sturtz. 1963. "The Manhattan Bail Project: An Interim Report on the Use of Pre-Trial Parole." *NYU Law Review* 38: 71–79, 81–92.

Barnsley, Jan. 1994. "Feminist Action, Institutional Reaction: Responses to Wife Assault." In Ronald Hinch (ed.), *Readings in Critical Criminology*. Scarborough, ON: Prentice.

Barss Donham, Parker. 1989. "The Ordeal of Donald Marshall." *Readers Digest*, September, 50–56 and October, 177–199.

Battle, Ken. 1998. "Poverty and the Welfare State." In Les Samuelson (ed.), *Power and Resistance: Critical Thinking about Canadian Social Issues*. 2nd edition. Halifax, NS: Fernwood.

Bell-Rowbotham, Beverly, and Craig L. Boydell. 1972. "Crime in Canada: A Distributional Analysis." In Craig Boydell, Carl F. Grindstaff, and Paul C. Whitehead (eds.), *Deviant Behaviour and Societal Reaction*. Toronto, ON: Holt.

Bedau, H.A. and M.L. Radelet. 1987. "Miscarriages of Justice in Potentially Capital Cases." *Stanford Law Review* 40: 21–179.

Bonger, Willem. 1967. *Criminality and Economic Conditions*. Boston, MA: Little.

Borchard, Edwin M. 1932. *Convicting the Innocent*. New Haven, CT: Yale University Press.

Burtch, Brian. 1981. "Reflections on the Steven Truscott Case." *Canadian Criminology Forum* 3(Spring): 131–45.

Canadian Broadcasting Corporation (Radio Network). 1985. "The Case of the Cowboy Killer." *The Scales of Justice*.

Canadian Broadcasting Corporation (Television Network). 1995a. "The Guy Paul Morin Case." *The Fifth Estate*, January 23.

_____. 1995b. "Jury Selection." *NewsWatch*, November 15.

Capital Case Files R.G. 1956. 13 Series. Wilbert Coffin 30. "Condensed Summary." Archives of Canada; Ottawa, ON.

CTV Television Network. 1986. *W-5 Program*. "The Thomas Sophonow Story." January 5.

Carvel, John. 1992. "Many Prisoners Could Be Wrongly Jailed." *Guardian Weekly*, April 5.

Chambliss, William J., and Robert B. Siedman. 1971. *Law Order and*

Power. Reading, MA: Wesley.

Clayton, Mark. 1995. "Captives of a Flawed Justice System." *Christian Science Monitor* March 27, 9–11.

Columbia Broadcasting System CBS (Television Network). 1997. *60 Minutes*. October.

Cunningham, Alison Hatch, and Curt T. Griffiths. 1997. *Canadian Criminal Justice: A Primer*. Toronto, ON: Harcourt.

Ericson, R.V., and P.M. Baranek. 1982. *The Ordering of Justice: A Study of Accused Persons as Dependents in the Criminal Process*. Toronto, ON: University of Toronto Press.

Fox, Vernon. 1976. *Introduction to Criminology*. Englewood Cliffs, NJ: Prentice.

Frank, Jerome, and Barbara Frank. 1957. *Not Guilty*. Garden City, NY: Doubleday.

Friedenberg, E.Z. 1980. "The Punishment Industry in Canada." *Canadian Journal of Sociology* 5(3): 273–83.

Friedland, Martin L. 1965. *Detention Before Trial: A Study of Criminal Cases Tried in the Toronto Magistrates' Courts*. Toronto, ON: University of Toronto Press.

Globe and Mail. 1995. "Picture Imperfect." January 21:D8.

Government of Nova Scotia. 1990. *Response to the Recommendations of the Royal Commission on the Donald Marshall Junior Prosecution*. Halifax, NS: February 7.

Hagan, John. 1977. *The Disreputable Pleasures*. Toronto, ON: McGraw.

Harding, Jim. 1991. "Policing and Aboriginal Justice." *Canadian Journal of Criminology* 33(3–4): 363–83.

Harris, Michael. 1986. *Justice Denied: The Law Versus Donald Marshall*. Toronto, ON: Harper-Collins.

Hastie, Reid, Stephen Penrod, and Nancy Pennington. 1983. *Inside the Jury*. Cambridge, MA: Harvard University Press.

Havemann, Paul. 1986. "Marketing the New Establishment Ideology in Canada." *Crime and Social Justice* 26:11–37.

Hebert, Jacques. 1964. *I Accuse the Assasins of Coffin*. Montreal, PQ: Les Editions.

Henderson, James "Sakej" Youngblood. 1992. "The Marshall Inquiry: A View of the Legal Consciousness." In Joy A. Manettte (ed.), *Elusive Justice*. Halifax, NS: Fernwood.

Hogarth, John. 1971. *Sentencing as a Human Process*. Toronto, ON: University of Toronto Press.

Huff, C. Ronald, Ayre Rattner, and Edward Sagarin. 1986. "Guilty Until Proven Innocent: Wrongful Convictions and Public Policy." *Crime and Delinquency* 32(4): 518–44.

———. 1996. *Convicted but Innocent: Wrongful Conviction and Public*

Policy. Thousand Oaks: Sage.

Hughes, Leslie. 1992. "A Mother Keeps Faith." *Chatelaine* April, 65–69, 182.

Hunter, Alfred. 1981. *Class Tells: On Social Inequality in Canada.* Toronto. ON: Butterworths.

Jenish, D'Arcy. 1992. "The Survivors." *Macleans* April 27, 46–48.

Karp, Carl, and Cecil Rosner. 1991. *When Justice Fails: The David Milgaard Story.* Toronto. ON: McClelland and Stewart.

Knuttila, Murray. 1996. *Introducing Sociology: A Critical Perspective.* Toronto, ON: Oxford University Press.

Law Reform Commission of Canada. 1974. *Discovery in Criminal Cases: Report on the Questionnaire Survey.* Ottawa, ON: Queen's Printer.

LeBourdais, Isabel. 1966. *The Trial of Steven Truscott.* Toronto, ON: McClelland and Stewart.

Logan, Alastair. 1995. "What Causes a Miscarriage of Justice?" *AIDWYC Journal* 1(1):6–9.

Loftus, Elizabeth. 1984. *Eyewitness Testimony: Psychological Perspectives.* Cambridge: Cambridge University Press.

Luus, C.A., and Gary L. Wells. 1994. "The Malleability of Eyewitness Confidence: Co-Witness and Perseverance Effects." *Journal of Applied Psychology* 79(5): 714–23.

Maclean, Brian. 1986. *The Political Economy of Crime.* Scarborough, ON: Prentice.

Makin, Kirk. 1992. *Redrum the Innocent.* Toronto, ON: Penguin.

_____. 1995. "What Was Missed of First Autopsy." *Globe and Mail* January 27.

Malloy, Ronald A. 1987. *Guilty Till Proven Innocent.* Toronto, ON: R.M.

Mandel, Michael. 1991. "Democracy, Class and Canadian Sentencing Law." In Elizabeth Comack and Stephen Brickley (eds.), *The Social Basis of Law: Critical Readings in the Sociology of Law.* Toronto, ON: Garamond.

Mannette, J.A. 1994. "Not Being a Part of the Way Things Work: Tribal Culture and Systematic Exclusion in the Donald Marshall Inquiry." In Ronald Hinch (ed.), *Readings in Critical Criminology.* Scarborough, ON: Prentice.

McMullan, John L. 1992. *Beyond the Limits of the Law.* Halifax, NS: Fernwood.

Myers, Martha. 1991. "A Structural and Judicial Discrimination in Sentencing." In Les Samuelson and Bernard Schissel (eds.), *Criminal Justice Sentencing Issues and Reform.* Toronto, ON: Garamound.

Panitch, Leo. 1977. "The Role and Nature of the Canadian State." In Panitch Leo (ed.), *The Canadian State: Political Economy and Political Power.* Toronto, ON: University of Toronto Press.

Petersen, Cynthia. 1993. "Institutionalized Racism: The Need for Reform of the Criminal Jury Selection Process." *McGill Law Journal* 38(1): 1.

Priest, Lisa. 1989. *Conspiracy of Silence*. Toronto, ON: McClelland and Stewart.

Quinney, Richard. 1970. *The Social Reality of Crime*. Boston, MA: Little.

Radelet, Michael L., Hugo Adam Bedeau, and Constance Putnam. 1992. *In Spite of Innocence: Erroneous Convictions in Capital Cases*. Boston, MA: Northeastern University Press.

Radelet, Michael L., Hugo Adam Bedeau, Constance Putnam, and Margaret Vandiver. 1986. "Race and Capital Punishment: An Overview of Issues." *Crime and Social Justice* 25: 94–113.

Ratner, Robert, John L. McMullan, and Brian E. Burtch. 1987. "The Problem of Relative Autonomy and Criminal Justice in the Canadian State." In Robert Ratner and John L. McMullan (eds.), *State Control: Criminal Justice Politics in Canada*. Vancouver, BC: University of British Columbia Press.

Rattner, Ayre. 1983. *Convicting the Innocent: When Justice Goes Wrong*. Unpublished Ph.D dissertation, Ohio State University.

_____. 1988. "Convicted but Innocent: Wrongful Convictions and the Criminal Justice System." *Law And Human Behaviour* 12(3): 283–93.

Regina Leader Post. 1992. "Crown Witness Admits to Lying." March 4.

_____. 1992. "Milgaard was Suspicious Character to Police." April 13:B5.

_____. 1992. "He Has Nowhere to Turn." April 17.

_____. 1992. "Milgaard Probe Ordered." November 17.

R v. Marshall. Nova Scotia Supreme Court. 1983. *Appeal Division Judgment*. May 10.

R. v. Truscott. (1967), C.R.N.S. 1 (S.C.C.); [1967] 2 C.C.C. 285 (S.C.C.).

Reiman, J. 1990. *The Rich Get Richer and the Poor Get Prison*. 3rd edition. New York, NY: Macmillan.

Rosen, Philip. 1992. *Wrongful Convictions in the Criminal Justice System*. Ottawa, ON: Library of Parliament Research Branch. BP 285E, January.

Ross, David, and Richard Shillington. 1989. *The Canadian Fact Book on Poverty, 1989*. Toronto, ON: Canadian Council on Social Development.

Royal Commission on the Donald Marshall, Junior Prosecution. 1990. *Commissioners' Report*. Halifax, Nova Scotia.

Scott, Robert, and Andrew Skull. 1978. "Penal Reform and the Surplus Army of Labour." In William K. Greenaway and Stephen L. Brickey (eds.), *Law and Social Control in Canada*. Scarborough, ON: Prentice.

Snider, Laureen. 1985. "Legal Aid, Reform, and the Welfare State." *Crime and Social Justice* 24: 210–42.

Stephens, Sam. 1991. "Aboriginal People and the Canadian Justice System." In Les Samuelson and Bernard Schissel (eds.), *Criminal Justice*

Sentencing Issues and Reform. Toronto, ON: Garamond.

Tarlow, Barry. 1995. "The Truth May Set You Free." *AIDWYC Journal* 1(1):16–19.

Tepperman, Lorne. 1977. *Crime Control.* Toronto, ON: McGraw.

Trent, Bill, and Stephen Truscott. 1979. *Who Killed Lynne Harper.* Ottawa, ON: Optimum.

Turk, Austin. 1969. *Criminality and the Legal Order.* Chicago, IL: Rand McNally.

USA Today. 1994. "Convicted on False Evidence?" July 19.

Wall, Bob. 1992. "Analyzing the Marshall Commission: Why It Was Established and How It Functioned." In Joy Mannette (ed.), *Elusive Justice: Beyond the Marshall Inquiry.* Halifax, NS: Fernwood.

Winnipeg Free Press. 1997. "Milgaard Case Points to Flaws." August 21, A8.

Yalnizyan, Armine. 1994. "Securing Society: Creating Canadian Social Policy." In Armine Yalnizyan, T. Ran Idle and Arthur Cordell (eds.), *Shifting Time: Social Policy and the Future of Work.* Toronto, ON: Between the Lines.

About the Authors

Barrie Anderson, professor emeritus, retired from the Department of Sociology at the University of Regina as an associate professor in 1996 after teaching the Sociology of Crime, Justice and Corrections for twenty years. Before becoming an academic he had worked as a labourer, truck driver, a nurse's aid in a psychiatric hospital, a game warden and a professional photographer. He was born and raised on the Canadian Prairies and presently lives in Regina with his wife and two children.

Dawn Anderson is a graduate student in Sociology at the University of Regina. Her main research interests include various topics within the Sociology of Crime. She is currently employed at the Sample Survey and Data Bank Unit at the University of Regina.